MISSIΟ

and

THE NEXT CHRISTENDOM

Papers read at the biennial conference of the
British and Irish Association for Mission Studies
at the Belfast Bible College, Northern Ireland
June 28 – July 1, 2005

Editor

Timothy Yates

cliff
COLLEGE
PUBLISHING

ISBN 1 898362 38 6
© 2005 Cliff College Publishing

British Library Cataloguing in Publication Data.
A catalogue record for this book is available
from the British Library.

**Cliff College Publishing,
Calver, Hope Valley, Nr Sheffield S32 3XG**

Printed by:

MOORLEY'S Print & Publishing
23 Park Rd., Ilkeston, Derbys DE7 5DA
Tel/Fax: (0115) 932 0643
from data supplied on electronically

CONTENTS

I. THE NEXT CHRISTENDOM?

II. ISSUES FOR EUROPE

III. GLOBAL PERSPECTIVES

Post-Colonialism

New Zealand

Latin America

CONTRIBUTORS

Valentin Dedji is a Methodist Minister from West Africa (Benin) working in Tottenham, London. He is author of *Reconstruction and Renewal in African Christian Theology*.

Darrell Jackson is a Baptist Minister working as a Research Officer for the Conference of European Churches in the field of mission and evangelism.

Viigo Mortensen is Professor of Global Christianity and Ecumenical Concerns in the University of Aarhus, where he is also Director of the Centre for Multi-Religious Studies. He is a contributing editor to *Theology and the Religions; a dialogue*.

Vinoth Ramachandra is a Secretary for Dialogue and Social Engagement (Asia) of the International Fellowship of Evangelical Students (IFES). He is from Sri Lanka and is author of *The Recovery of Mission* and *Faiths in Conflict?*

Kathy Ross is a New Zealander, who holds a doctorate in mission history from the University of Auckland. She has recently joined the staff of the Church Mission Society (CMS) in the UK.

Stephen Skuce is Post-Graduate Tutor for Mission Studies at Cliff College, now affiliated to the University of Manchester.

Stephen Spencer is the Principal of the Northern Ordination Course. He has previously served in Zimbabwe and is currently the Publications Secretary of BIAMS and editor of its bi-annual bulletin.

Werner Ustorf is Professor of Mission and Director of the Centre for Missiology and World Christianity in the University of Birmingham. He is author of *Sailing on the Next Tide: Missiology and the Third Reich* and a contributing editor to *The Decline of Christendom in Western Europe 1750-2000*.

Allan Yeh is a research student at the University of Oxford.

The British and Irish Association for Mission Studies is an inter-confessional body founded in 1990 as a forum for both academic teachers and missionary practitioners and others interested in mission.

It publishes a twice-yearly newsletter and holds day conferences and biennial residential conferences.

Details of membership can be obtained from the Secretary,
C/o The Henry Martyn Centre,
Westminster College,
Cambridge CB3 0AA
or from the website
http://www.martynmission.cam.ac.uk/BIAMSConf.htm

FOREWORD

Philip Jenkins published the book *The Next Christendom: the Coming of Global Christianity* in 2002. The executive of the British and Irish Association of Mission Studies (BIAMS) were first made aware of the book by its then Chairman, Dr Larry Nemer SVD, after a visit he had paid to his previous teaching setting at the Catholic Theological Union in Chicago. Here he had found other theologians and missiologists excited and stimulated by the book. In due course his successor in the Chair of BIAMS, Dr Kirsteen Kim, with her colleagues on the Executive, decided to plan a residential conference, which aimed to respond to the challenges offered by the book towards the future of Christianity. Professor Werner Ustorf from Birmingham and Dr Vinoth Ramachandra from Sri Lanka and Dr Valentin Dedji originally from West Africa and others were invited to bring European, Asian and African perspectives to bear with their critical insights into the material.

Although Philip Jenkins emphasises that no such doomsday scenario is a determined necessity, his book raises the spectre of Christian crusade confronting Muslim *jihad*, the possibility of an increasingly fundamentalist church of the south confronting a militant and radical Islam. As he peered into the future, extrapolating from present trends, his estimate of Christian strength for 2025 in terms of continents caused Europe to slip to third place in the world Christian populations behind Africa (633 million Christians), Latin America (640 million) with Europe at 555 million, still however larger than Asia in Christian presence, at 460 million. He discounted, however, predictions that Islam would overtake Christianity in world population. By contrast, he estimated that in 2050 there would be three Christians for every two Muslims and that Christians would make up 34% of the world population (p.5). He has conceded the speculative nature of such calculations, basing them on figures released by the US Government and the statistics available in the *World Christian Encyclopaedia* of 2001 (pp.223-4).

The conference at which these papers were read took place over June 28th-July 1st 2005 in the hospitable circumstances of the Belfast Bible College. It is hoped that the considerable intellectual stimulus

7

gained there will be welcomed more widely. We are grateful to Cliff College, providers of mission studies now through the University of Manchester, for agreeing to make these papers available to a wider audience. It is our hope that *Mission and the Next Christendom* will be a helpful and thought-provoking successor to its three preceding volumes from the same source: *Mission – An Invitation to God's Future* (2000), *Mission and Spirituality* (2002) and *Mission, Violence and Reconciliation* (2004).

Timothy Yates

Part I

THE NEXT CHRISTENDOM

WHY CHRISTENDOM IS AN UNLIKELY CANDIDATE FOR CHRISTIANITY'S FUTURE

Werner Ustorf

1. Philip Jenkins, who by profession is a historian of religion at Pennsylvania State University and, by denomination, an Episcopalian, has distinguished himself as a critical public voice in American society and culture. He has published books on the controversial issues of pornography and paedophilia.[1] He is particularly critical of American Christianity. With reference to the Catholic Church, for example, he discovered that there existed "widespread sexual misconduct" within the clergy and that there was widespread clerical contempt for the interests of the laity. There can be no doubt that, for Jenkins, sexual misconduct in all its forms is a highly symbolic landmark and indicative of the decline of the Church in the West. On the other hand, he also criticized the generally accepted anti-Catholic bias in American politics and culture.[2] Jenkins distributes his criticism quite evenly, and always with great sensitivity regarding the wider ramifications of public discussion. These considerations are also true of his provocative 2002 book on the *Next Christendom*,[3] a work that rolls missiology, history, demography and geopolitics into one. At the same time it represents a formidable critique of liberal Christianity. I am a

---

1   *Beyond Tolerance: Child Pornography on the Internet*, New York: New York University Press, 2001, and *Pedophiles and Priests: Anatomy of a Contemporary Crisis*, New York: OUP, 1996. Sexual abuse features only once (65) in his *The Next Christendom*.
2   *The New Anti-Catholicism. The Last Acceptable Prejudice*, New York: OUP, 2004.
3   I will abbreviate the title as *The Next Christendom*.

historian, a missiologist and a liberal Christian and I am experiencing difficulties with at least some of the more provocative ideas with which Jenkins is challenging us. I will briefly summarize and discuss the big picture Jenkins is offering and, then, engage in a more political conversation with him.

2. Jenkins, in a scenario first outlined in 1999,[4] and slightly less dramatic in a response to his critics published in 2004 in the *International Bulletin of Missionary Research*,[5] says that in the last decades Christianity has mutated into a religion of the South, and that in the decades to come, North Atlantic Christianity will be a small – and rather odd - minority undertaking within the shadow of its southern counterpart. In particular, European Christianity will be sustained mainly by southern immigrants. In his alarming overview of World Christianity in *The Atlantic Monthly* of October 2002,[6] Jenkins went further than he did in the book and described the situation of the Christian faith in the West today as being as bad as it was in the years immediately preceding 1517, and that another reformation was inevitable. This time, however, the reforming power and the authenticity of faith would come from the South, and it would certainly not fulfil the dreams of Western intellectuals. Rather, it would turn back the clock of history and be as theocratic, intolerant, crusading and credulous as the Taliban regime has been or, for that matter, the city-states of Zurich or Geneva in the 16th century. I think that Salman Rushdie is right in claiming that every writer's unfettered vision of the world generates a truth.[7] Here, we do have such an unfettered vision. Of course, there are weaknesses. Specialists might wish, for example, to take issue with the statistical foundation of the argument, usually based on data provided by David Barrett's *World Christian Encyclopaedia* and by the forecasts of US intelligence agencies, or, again, they may baulk at his tendency to generalize.[8] Jenkins – in the

---

4   *That New Time Religion*, in: *Chronicles: A Magazine of American Culture*, August 1999, 17-19. This information is based on Jenkins' *The Next Christendom*.

5   After the Next Christendom, in: *IBMR* 28(1), 2004, 20-22.

6   Pp. 53-68. Interestingly, the title is here *The Next Christianity*; I have taken the text was from http://www.theatlantic.com/doc/prem/200210/jenkins, April 2005. The article is in fact a rewrite of the first chapter of his book, *The Next Christendom. The Coming of Global Christianity*, Oxford and New York: OUP, 2002.

7   Rushdie in: *The Guardian*, 23rd April 2005.

8   Labels such as the "global North" and the "global South" are handy umbrella terms and useful as long as they simply refer to a large body of knowledge. When applied in

interest of his *big picture* – has indeed introduced a rigorous distinction between a "northern" and a "southern" form of Christian experience. I think he went too far when he characterized the hungry embrace of orthodox Christianity (including its opposition to the ordination of women priests or the tolerance of homosexuality), and the expectation of God's direct intervention in a life that is troubled by alienation and demonic forces as a specifically *southern* phenomenon. There is also too much simplification in the claim that the *northern* experience is characterized by a selective process, according to which belief is admitted only if it fits into the modern liberal mythology, a process leading finally to the abandonment of the faith. The problem is that the truth contained in this vision becomes invisible behind this screen of geographical reductionism. Jenkins has his own agenda and tends to portray a large chunk of western Christian experience as being like the one rotten apple on an otherwise healthy though not really tempting tree. He invites us to follow his agenda. But his constant preaching against "Northern liberals" and their "dilettantish kind of cafeteria religion" (197) and his cautious fascination with the "exotic beast" of Southern "jungle religion" (162, 220) seriously damages his argument. The questions I have do not arise so much from the individual statistical or historical data that Jenkins uses,[9] but rather from the wrapper they are in, that is, from a set of generalizations that work in a particular direction.

One of my questions relates to the Christian experience of the South. Jenkins depicts it as a spiritual experience of liberation, healing and community building, as well as a religious way of dealing with oppression, illness and homelessness, including exorcism. Such spiritual experience draws much its power from the fact that it is

---

analysis they lose their usefulness because they suggest a uniformity that is actually not there. Jenkins is aware of this.

9   For three decades missiologists tried to draw attention to the demographic and theological shifts in world Christianity, perhaps in vain. The phenomenal growth of this religion after the end of colonialism – and in the presence of modernization – should have blown the secular bias of the western academy out of the water. However, the public preferred to look the other way. Therefore, Jenkins is absolutely right for bringing these facts to the attention of a wider public. In general, he is also right in his estimates and, based on very wide reading, shows a convincing picture of Christianity's journey through history. His point that the average Christian in the 13th century was from Syria or Mesopotamia, rather than from France, is well made. We all have probably grown up with a heavily Europeanized view of Christian history. There can also be no question that the predicted massive urbanization in the growth areas of the South, together with the social and identity issues that accompany it, will be of crucial importance for the future global balance of religion.

embedded within a given social and cultural context and, also, that it has often sought a syncretistic merger with pre-existing folk religion. In general, of course, these observations are quite right, and had Jenkins said that such religious practice was really no more than a set of structured illusions, then his views would in fact have coincided with Karl Marx's definition of religion. But he does not say this. Southern Christianity, instead is seen as a fairly seamless extension to the normal warp and weft of biblical narrative. The historian becomes an armchair theologian and, as a result, uses the adjective "fundamentalist" to describe what he sees as the re-enactment of the gospels. If one accepts this description and combines it with the accepted forecast of global demography, then the conclusion is almost inevitable: we are heading irreversibly towards a world in which liberal Western Christianity is in steep and almost terminal decline, while its fundamentalist Southern counterpart is triumphantly in the ascendant. This may be frightening enough, but Jenkins scares us further by insisting that the fundamentalist South has a predilection for violence, anti-Semitism and that it one day might embark on a new crusade against an equally third-worldly religion, namely, a fundamentalist and jihadic Islam. I shall return to the political dimensions of this in a moment.

The individual historical arguments then have some force, but I am not comfortable with the overall picture. *Firstly*, if the principle of contextuality is applied to the South, it ought to be applied to the North as well. There is no discussion of the context of the *global North*. Is Christian faith possible in the North? We may ask, quite legitimately, what would, could or must Christianity look like if it were to be inculturated in a late-capitalist Western society? This is something I want to address in my other paper. *Secondly*, is the southern Christian experience, by definition, fundamentalist – that is the gospel narratives played before our eyes? For example, any attempt at painting the self-confident Kimbanguists in Central Africa with the brush of fundamentalism would be misleading. After the independence of the Congo in 1960, one of the first acts of the Kimbanguist Church was to liaise with the ecumenical movement and, later, in the 1970s, it established a faculty of Kimbanguist theology. The idea behind this was not to preserve and defend a Kimbanguist *depositum fidei*, because that did not yet exist. The real point was to develop a theology that was capable of expressing the church's historical and spiritual

12

experiences in terms that were African but also ecumenical. To be critical of the West, and the Kimbanguists surely are, is not the same as being fundamentalist or theologically autistic. An African Independent Church that works theologically is also a church that has been driven from paradise: it has lost the immediacy and innocence of the original event and begins to share the problem common to all theology from the days of St. Paul on: theology in its search for God is only a pointer to what it itself is not. Theology helps *faith* to face this problem – in Africa and in Europe. My information is that Christian voices in the South are various, diverse, and distinct.[10] There may be as much theological disagreement as we have in the "global North". Theological disagreement, and the sprouting of one or two heresies, to quote Hans Hoekendijk, are signs of theological maturity. The maturity of the Christians in the South is something Jenkins concedes as a possibility only in the future. I am finding, on the other hand, evidence of that maturity right now. We call it theology. And because of this the global South will no doubt continue to criticize the West, but it is highly unlikely that it will go on the rampage or proceed helter-skelter down the road that Jenkins has prepared for it.

4. Let us look now at the political dimensions of this scenario. Jenkins is entitled to criticize the churches of the West for paying too little attention to the possibility that Christianity's battle for supremacy in the world market of religion might be won or lost in the mega-cities of the South, as opposed to those in the North. He predicts, for example, that a religion that "builds there today is very likely to be profiting richly in a decade or two." I must confess that I have my doubts as to whether this is true, and whether Christianity can "dominate the religious economy" (212) by missionary intervention alone.[11] Jenkins warns that the dominating religion of the future might not be Christianity, but, perhaps, Islam. What is worse, the Christian West, or what is left of it, seems to be actively pursuing a policy of

---

10 For an overview see the *SCM Dictionary of Third World Theologies*, ed. by V. Fabella and R.S. Sugirtharajah, London: SCM, 2003.
11 The fact is that, despite the truly massive missionary efforts of the 20th century, the relative share of Christianity in the world's population has not changed in the last one hundred years. I am also not so sure that Western mission agencies need to hear lessons like this, because the *out-sourcing* of mission structures from the North to the South is already taking place, often driven by financial considerations. Quite a number of classical mission agencies have transformed themselves into interchurch-agencies, spanning North and South and experimenting with resource allocation that is based on the principle of equality.

religious self-destruction. All of this is reminiscent of Samuel Huntington, who also deploys the minatory image of *the enemy is inside the walls*. Referring to the crisis in Kossovo in 1999, Jenkins says:

"The net result of the Allied intervention was a massive advance of Muslim power and militancy within south-eastern Europe, at the expense of ancient Christian communities. At the same time, the oppressed Christians of the Sudan were receiving no support from NATO, or any Western or Christian entity. Even mainstream Western churches were unwilling to be too forthright in denouncing persecution. For Konrad Raiser, head of the World Council of Churches, the main lesson of the massacres in Indonesia and Nigeria was that Christians needed to reassess their missionary endeavours, to avoid causing offence to other cultures." (186).

This means, to stay within Jenkins' perspective for a moment, that the religious battle lines must not only be controlled by the West, they must also be drawn very clearly within its own borders.[12] At which point, perhaps, we should confront the argument that a dominant, but also fundamentalist and even "reactionary" and "fanatic" Southern Christianity[13] will somehow merge into an "axis" of global *Christendom*. This implies that passionate religious identification takes precedence over any allegiance to the secular political order, such as that of a nation-state. We have heard this before, of course, from Huntington and a number of other scholars.[14] The focus of loyalty, it is said, is not the individual state, but the overarching unity of an imagined sacred empire. Jenkins speculates, using Max Weber's and Ernst Troeltsch's typology of church and sect, as to whether, in the distant future, this seething cauldron of turmoil will simply boil to nothing, leaving, as it were, a residue in which Southern Christendom again becomes a plurality of churches. But, for the foreseeable future, the religious imagination of the South would have serious and direct political consequences: in practice, some form of crusading theocracy

---

12 It matters, for example, whether churches are interested in or indifferent to the teaching of theology in western universities. To stay with my own university, Birmingham, I have to say that it is currently not the Christian but the other faith traditions that are investing heavily in its *Department of Theology and Religion*. The likelihood is that a concentration of Christian personnel and money in the South, at the expense of the North, is not a panacea.

13 Jenkins used these terms in *The New Christendom*.

14 Cp. for example S. Rudolph, *Transnational Religion and Fading States*, Bolder, Colorado: Westview, 1997.

engaged in a series of violent conflicts with Islam, but carried out with modern weapons. The structures of this Christendom, Jenkins thinks, however, would have much in common with those Europe had exhibited in the past, particularly during the Middle Ages.

Why Southern Christianity, with its varieties of distinctly different cultural, religious, and contextual backgrounds, should follow a medieval European trajectory is not clear.[15] However, I do not think that Jenkins is using the idea of *Christendom* as a tool of historical analysis. He has tried instead to find an analogy that is capable of providing his *nightmare scenarios* with some measure of historical credibility.[16] I do not think that the analogy is a happy one. The *nightmare* Jenkins is conjuring up has little to do with the *res publica christiana* of the Middle Ages, with its dual dispensation in the shape of *imperium* and *sacerdotum*. What he is depicting is in fact a phenomenon of recent, not medieval, religious history, which is to say, the post-western removal of the distinction between the political and the religious, as Huntington has already stated to be the case for the 20th century. A characteristic of totalitarian religion is its amalgamation of the two realms. There are two ways for the achievement of this amalgamation, which can be distinguished theoretically, though less easily in practice: one is the sacralization of the political. The sacralization of the political, in its most serious and destructive form, occurred in the 20th century, in the shape of political religions such as Nazism, and this, of course, happened at the heart of Europe. The other way is the nightmare that Jenkins describes under the banner of medieval Christendom, namely, the politicization of the sacred.[17]

Such a species of Christianity, if it were to come, would inevitably run into immediate theological trouble, just as other forms of politicized religion had. The kind of theological critique that must be made against it can be gleaned, for example, from the way theologians

---

15 It is also not clear whether the South alone would be responsible for the decline of the nation-state. Jenkins himself argues that factors generated in the West, such as information technology, markets, globalization or the emergence of the European Union, are anyway busy in eroding the sense of belonging to a particular state.

16 *Nightmare* is a term used by Jenkins himself.

17 For terminology cp. Emilio Gentile, The Sacralisation of Politics: Definitions, Interpretations and Reflections on the Question of Secular Religion, in: *Totalitarian Movements and Political Religions*, 1/1 (2000); idem, *The Sacralization of Politics in Fascist Italy*, Cambridge, MA: Harvard UP, 1996.

in the 1930s dealt with the politicization of religion that happened in their time. Paul Tillich and Karl Barth could be quoted here. However, the critical concept of "political religion" was actually developed by missiologists, who used it at the time as a form of theological weapon. It was first coined by the Lutheran missiologist and, later, professor of theology, Paul Schütz (1891-1985). Like many missionaries, he had discovered on the mission field that a new kind of western creed had undermined Christianity's credibility. In 1932, Schütz published a full study of what he then called *Secular Religion*; and in 1935 he added a manuscript entitled *Political Religion*.[18] What Schütz had to say is, briefly, this:

Christianity in the West is, as a consequence of the collapse of liberal-occidental culture, mutating into a secular religion. With their faith dissolved, the inner emptiness of the masses and their hunger for certainty provided fertile ground for a new political creed. What secular or political religion does is to take the sacred out of the old faith and put it into secular and political life. Christianity becomes secular or political when its believers claim Paradise, the Kingdom of God, and the Resurrection for their imagined political-religious empire. Secular religion embraces falsity because it is unwilling to wake up to the "true situation"; that is, to respect the otherness of God and the hiddenness of Truth, and to accept our aphasia, our speechlessness in these matters. Instead, secular religion speaks unhesitatingly of God, Truth, humanity and history, denying that these are purely self-generated images. Secular religion, therefore, is the dialectical amalgamation of *reality*, which is God's, and an *interpretation*, which is ours. This amalgamation is sinful because it removes the distance between the two. Ultimately, it makes God an attribute of man, and heaven a place on earth. Secular religion, in the end, is spiritual rebellion against God. It is violent by nature and contains the recipe for its own destruction. Violence and conflict are the inevitable outcome of its religious vision, which demands the merger of God and man and of eternity and history. Its mode of believing is therefore not *faith*, but *obsession*.

---

18 Cp. his *Säkulare Religion. Eine Studie über ihre Erscheinung in der Gegenwart und ihre Idee bei Schleiermacher und Blumhardt d.J.*, Tübingen: Mohr Siebeck, 1932; and idem, *Die politische Religion. Eine Untersuchung über den Urpsrung des Verfalls in der Geschichte*, unpublished, typed manuscript (63 pp.), 1935. The manuscript is held by Staatsarchiv Hamburg, 622-1, Familie Paul Schütz, 248.

Totalitarianism would not be any less disastrous if it came along in Christian garments, whether these originated in the South or the North. A new Christendom of the fanatical kind is the last thing this world needs; it is theologically wrong, and it has to be avoided. If Jenkins is right, theologians everywhere have to stand up and be counted. In my view, however, the Christian *global South*, is not on this road. If something like a "theocratic absolutism" is under way, to quote the writer Philip Pullman, it is more likely to come out of Tony Blair's Britain, where there is a trend to let "obnoxiously superstitious and self-righteous" people have their way.[19] Very few of the examples quoted by Jenkins could in any case be classified as a politicization of the sacred. Instead, he throws sometimes completely heterogeneous political phenomena into a single conceptual basket: politicians manipulating religious bodies, self-styled messiahs meting out apocalyptic violence, Church leaders challenging the political authorities in the area of human rights, or churches offering a kind of parallel administration in states where the infrastructure has collapsed. Such examples, valuable as they are individually, are in no way supportive of his thesis of a global southern trend towards a "political ideology" of Christendom or the emergence of a violent "theocratic Christian state".[20] These are just nightmares, projections perhaps. But where did they come from in the first place? There is of course the dark history of Europe's 20th century, with its violence and sacralized totalitarian ideology. More recently, there is politicized Islam, also very much prepared for violence. Finally, we have the neo-conservatism of the Christian Right in the US – and it is currently part of America's discourse of power. Their sacred vision is extremely frightening to many. All this seems to me to be the stuff of nightmares. It is almost, though, as if Jenkins has sought to exorcise these demons by projecting them on to the South.

On the basis of this, I have decided to take the Jenkins scenario as a political manifesto. Jenkins addresses his ideas explicitly to "our political leaders and diplomats".[21] These must be, in the first place, the makers of US foreign policy. In other words, this very influential study is not simply the academic exercise of a disinterested historian, it is meant to have an impact on the discourse on policy and strategy of

---

19 Pullman in *The Times Higher Education*, 22 April 2005, 18-19.
20 *Next Christendom*, 141-159.
21 *The Next Christendom*, 13.

the leading world power. If I were a sort of youngish Henry Kissinger, I would hear Jenkins say the following:

> The continuation of the role of the US as a leading world power is dependent on more than oil and military force. As an empire that is shaped by Christianity it requires an uncompromising religious vision and must bring this to bear in the global religious conflicts of the future. This empire can no longer rely on Europe because, in the future, parts of it either go mainly Muslim, stay mainly secular or, as in the case of Britain, will have a majority derived from the Third World and, therefore, will become a form of religious   fault line. The main conflict will be between Christianity and Islam. This conflict may result in global wars that will originate in the Third World. The US can deflect their impact by doing two things: be ideologically in agreement with southern Christianity, by marginalizing liberal forms of Christianity at home, and by supporting southern Christianity in the urban centres of the Third World.[22]

I repeat, this is not what Jenkins is saying, it is what I am hearing. However, the idea at the heart of this scenario is that there are solid and insurmountable boundaries between religions and cultures. This idea is itself an idea with a history. The syncretistic origins of all religions and the actual lives of the people on the ground continuously keep falsifying this idea, but because it is related intimately with power it has been around for quite a while. Its more recent history is largely connected with the global expansion of the West and its encounter with profound diversity. Part of this process was Western scholarship, with its analysis and classification of "otherness", that is to say, with the introduction of boundaries. Without such boundaries the conceptualization of otherness and of "us" and "them" was hardly possible. These sharp boundaries found their way into the textbooks of the world, but, even after these reifications of closed identity have become a large part of the self-understanding of the major religions, historically they are also related to the Western imagination. This imagination, however, whether Christian or secular, was not innocent, because it played a central part in the process of Western expansion,

---

22 Interestingly, Tony Blair – after the no-vote in France and the Netherlands on the European Constitution and addressing his imminent talks with George Bush – is said to have made the remark "Africa is worth fighting for. Europe, in its present form, is not." Quoted in *The Sunday Telegraph*, 5th of June, 2005, page 1.

that is, it was part of a discourse that functioned in the interest of Western power, politics, commerce and exploration. The empire needed this imagination for its spiritual upkeep, but no less for its military advance. If there is incommunication in principle between the diversity of religious and cultural identities, you do not mix, rather, you calculate, study and, in the case of Western expansion, dominate and control the "other", or, in the best case, you convert the other to what you think you yourself are. The question was, as Humpty Dumpty said in Lewis Carroll's *Through the Looking Glass*, "which is to be master – that is all."[23]

In times like ours, when diversity has become an established fact of life, the new empire must be in a constant state of turmoil: it has become increasingly difficult to maintain rigid religious and cultural boundaries, yet the empire's geopolitical and economic demands require a strong imagination or vision. Jenkins offers just such a vision, comprising a sophisticated imagination, but involving as well a tightening up of core religious values in the United States. But this geopolitical dimension makes me wish to locate Jenkins' approach on a larger map. To do this, I have chosen three cultural critics of the West, all of whom proved to be highly influential in shaping public opinion as regards the global cultural process – Oswald Spengler, Francis Fukuyama and Samuel Huntington. Only Huntington is used extensively by Jenkins, but Huntington consulted Spengler and Fukuyama, and all three throw a most interesting light on Jenkins.

Let me begin with Spengler, the sceptical German cultural philosopher and critic of modern capitalism and technology. Spengler was at home in conservative-revolutionary circles and wrote his magnum opus during the Great War. The two volumes of his *The Decline of the West* were published in 1918 and 1922.[24] Here, Spengler defined Western civilization as an "exceptional case and not the rule" – requiring a Copernican revolution in the notion of world history.[25] There were no universal concepts. World history was rather a series of eight large cultures (or, in their late stage, "civilizations") – India, Babylon, China, Egypt, the Mexican and the Arabian cultures,

---

23 Cp. also W. Cantwell Smith, *The Meaning and End of Religion*, London: SPCK, 1978.
24 *Der Untergang des Abendlandes. Umrisse einer Morphologie der Weltgeschichte*. I have used the following edition, Munich: Beck, 1923 (vol. I, 47th edition) and 1922 (vol. II, 42nd edition).
25 Vol. I, 20, 34.

classical antiquity and western culture. None was privileged and each of them had its own distinct "soul" and therefore existed in complete independence of the others.[26] Among these civilizations cultural incommunication ruled. Civilizations were incommensurable and incompatible. We have seen that incommunication of this sort also plays a role in Jenkins' approach. Jenkins holds that the Christian *North* and the Christian *South* are incapable of understanding each other.[27] In Spengler's view, all civilizations, independently of their character, were subjected to the same evolutionary or organological laws; namely the cycles of spring, summer, autumn and winter and of birth, youth, adulthood and old age. This biological analogy enabled him to make fascinating comparisons of the different phases of cultural development across a spectrum of cultures. Now, the whole point of Spengler's comparative method was to predict world history and this is another thing that Jenkins has in common with him. The leading world civilization at the time was, according to Spengler, the industrialized West. However, it was "exhausted", like the Roman Empire of the fourth century, and appeared to be sliding into its last stage, which Spengler defined as "late civilization", characterized in this case by swollen mega-cities and the spread of imperialism across the globe. All of this meant that the West was wasting its energy and spirit in its attempts to dominate the periphery, while emptiness was rising in the centre. Its originality began to dry up and irreligion, a post-liberal spirituality that Spengler calls the "second religiosity" of wishful credulity, primitive religion and popular syncretism, was on the march.[28] Like the Roman Empire, modern western civilization would end in a kind of dictatorship, before, as a denouement, giving way to the invaders. Jenkins is still doing battle with liberalism, and we shall see why.

Fukuyama's article *The End of History and the Last Man?* was published in 1989 in the journal *The National Interest*, while the book of the same title – omitting the question-mark – appeared in 1992.[29]

---

26 This is the reason why it did not make sense to apply Western categories and concepts to the Chinese or Indian or any other non-Western civilization. For example, the traditional periodisation of European history - antiquity, middle age, and modernity – did not make sense elsewhere.

27 *Next Christendom*, 160 f.

28 Vol. II, 382 f.

29 *The National Interest*, no 16, 3-18. I used the following book edition, London: Penguin, 1992.

His book represents an unashamed and full return to the universalist ideas of the Enlightenment, in marked contrast to Spengler. Fukuyama was then a member of the US State Department's Policy Planning Staff, and the two publications, very much like Jenkins' book, are addressed to politicians. His extravagant and overtly optimistic thesis, as is well known, is that after the fall of communism liberal democracy has not just outlived any other system of government, it had in fact become the ultimate form of human government. It is ultimate because liberal democracy fully implements the twin principles of liberty and equality and, therefore, constitutes the end of history. He got it ostentatiously wrong. It has to be said on Fukuyama's behalf, however, that his teleological argument is not a historical, but a philosophical one. Based on Hegel's *Philosophy of History* and the important chapter on domination and slavery in the same author's *Phenomenology of Mind*, Fukuyama defines "the desire for recognition" as the driving force of all human history. Liberal democracy had found a formula in which everybody was recognized. It had, therefore, in principle at least, resolved the contradiction of master and slave and had removed any wish for domination or the need for revolution, for nationalistic strife, and for theocracies and totalitarianism. History would cease in the "post-historical period", an era suspiciously close to Spengler's description of the moral and intellectual decline in "late civilization". Fukuyama is, it has to be said, worried by the potential for boredom and mediocrity that is implicit in this scenario. But, this may be the price he has to pay for not having bothered to explain how Fascism could arise inside a liberal democracy, and, as another grievous omission, for not having included the continent of Africa in his book. Islam is included, and is identified as a real competitor to liberal democracy, at least within its cultural borders. But, eventually, it too would succumb to the overwhelming forces of liberal democracy.[30] Christianity is an altogether different matter, because Fukuyama sees it, along with Nietzsche, as somehow otherworldly and, in any case, as a religion of the victorious slave.[31] Christianity has the right kind of idea about human freedom, but argues that such freedom is available only in another world. Therefore, Christianity is no competitor at all; but, more than this, liberal democracy is its secularized form and has taken over and completed

30 *End of History*, 45 f.
31 Ibid., 197 ff., 301 ff.

the Christian heritage. Jenkins would strongly disagree with this, in particular with regard to his views of the *global South*.

This scenario of universal history and rationality, the "illusion of harmony", with its unfettered westernness and its disregard for the world's cultures and religions is what Huntington attacked a year later. Huntington had been Fukuyama's tutor at Harvard. He, like Jenkins, wants to be considered a realist. In 1993 he published his famous article *The Clash of Civilizations?* in the semi-official journal *Foreign Affairs*, followed in 1996 by a book of the same title – and, again, the question-mark has gone.[32] His well-known advice to the US foreign policy makers is always to keep in mind that violent conflicts between the world's leading civilizations are inevitable, whether these be local "fault-line wars" or major global confrontations. The dream of a universal civilization based on rationality, as embodied in the United Nations for example, was over and a return of the irrational, the religious and the sacred, in brief, chaos, was once again on the cards. This resonates with Spengler and, of course, with Jenkins. For Huntington the world is divided in a familiar "West and the rest" manner. The West is seen as fundamentally different from the rest. Unlike Jenkins, however, but in common with Spengler, Huntington does not speak as such of the global South, but instead highlights the existence of eight very diverse civilizations outside the West: Latin American, African, Islamic, Sinic, Hindu, Slavonic-Orthodox (interestingly), Buddhist and Japanese. This is not the place to discuss this, but the point is made that Huntington, like Spengler, excludes any possibility of intercultural learning or, if you will, the natural give and take between cultures. Huntington predicts not only a comprehensive decline in the importance of the West, but also forecasts dangerous conflicts taking place not so much between social classes or the rich and the poor, and not even between nation-states, but between peoples espousing different cultural and religious identities. It is important to understand that, for Huntington, religion is the defining element of a civilization. Therefore, Christianity should be crucial for both the definition and the survival of Western civilization.[33] All the same, he identifies no specific category of *Christian* civilization. The reason

---

32 *The Clash of Civilizations and the Remaking of World Order*. I have used the following edition, London and New York: Touchstone Books, 1998. On pp. 31 and 66 Huntington directly confronts Fukuyama.
33 Ibid., 305.

seems to be that, for a millennium or more, that is before it went through its modernization, Western civilization was a mix of traditions inherited from previous civilizations: there is, for example, Greek philosophy and rationalism, Roman law, Latin and, as just one of many factors, Christianity.[34]   What distinguishes the West from other civilizations, therefore, is not modernization but this particular mix or cultural inheritance, which includes the phenomena of the separation of religion and politics or, if you will, of spiritual and temporal authority - "an idiosyncratic product of Western civilization", as Huntington would have it.[35]   With the decline of the West, this separation would also decline and result in the intrusion of religion into international politics. Jenkins' work complements this line of thought, but there is also a major point of departure here in that he adds to Huntington's overview the missing *civilization*, of *global Christianity*. By focussing on the Catholic, Protestant and Pentecostal sections of this religion he shows that a massive fault-line runs through it – one third belonging to the declining West, two thirds or thereabouts to the rising rest. In other words, Jenkins is saying what many critics have also said, that most conflicts are not between civilizations but *within* them. But he also goes beyond Huntington, by stating that the Christianity of the *global South* no longer shares the core values of western mainstream Christianity. But all the other elements of Jenkins' approach, the focus on the shifts in global demography, the prediction that Islam and Christianity will battle it out in the new growth areas, are established themes in Huntington's work. Like Jenkins, and Spengler, Huntington, in his last chapter, deplores the moral decline in the West. The internal self-destruction leads to a stage where Western civilization is no longer willing to defend itself and is wide open to "barbarian invaders". But these invaders have already arrived in the shape of "a small but influential number of intellectuals and publicists. In the name of multiculturalism they have … denied the existence of a common American culture, and promoted racial, ethnic, and other subnational cultural identities and groupings."[36]   This kind of development, if unchecked, could destroy Western civilization. Jenkins follows this

---

34   Ibid., 69.
35   Ibid., 54.
36   Ibid., 305.

decline of the West narrative, but he does not seem to be worried about the *barbarian invaders* as long as they are *Christian*.[37]

There can be no question that all the *big pictures* drawn by Spengler, Fukuyama, Huntington and Jenkins, are determinist and reductionist. It is conceivable that this is the price that must be paid for any *grand narrative*. For us, however, it is of greater significance that they all presuppose that different cultures and, more importantly still, the Christians of the North and the South, are incapable of talking to and learning from one another. It is this very fact, however, this unwillingness to talk and to learn, that is the logical precondition for the conflict and war that are so central to all of the above narratives.

World Christianity is indeed facing many conflicts. There is also a conflict of theological interpretation that needs to be resolved. But this conflict is not so much between the declining Christianity of the not so liberal West and its growing fundamentalist counterpart in the South, it is much more about *Christianity* per se, that is, as a universalistic religious ideology, and *Christianness* as a way of life. Christians ought to give Caesar his due, but that does not mean that we have to swallow his political imagination hook, line and sinker. The boundaries around Christianity must not be made subservient to political interests and it is important to resist the Siren songs we are hearing from Philip Jenkins. We need to rethink the boundary question in the light of a new worldwide context. Raymondo Panikkar has suggested that we should distinguish between different stages in the learning process of the Christian tradition: a path that takes us from Christendom, and, then, via Christianity to Christianness.[38]

---

37 The British journalist Francis Wheen, when commenting on "the binary simplicity" of Fukuyama and Huntington, asked whether both had taken the same correspondence course on *How to Be a Modern Political Guru in Three Easy Lessons*: first, summarise your tentative thesis in an American policy journal. Secondly, devise a concept so arrestingly simple "that it can be understood and discussed even by half-witted politicians or TV chat-show hosts." Thirdly, having got everyone talking about your provocative new idea, reap the rewards by expanding it into a best-selling book. Francis Wheen, *How Mumbo-Jumbo Conquered the World*, London: Harper, 2004, 70 f. Wheen could not know that in 2005 the superstar economic advisor to 100 governments, Jeffrey Sachs, would publish his *The End of Poverty: Economic Possibilities for Our Time*, Penguin Press (USA). Sachs claimed here that the world's extreme poverty could be eradicated within 20 years by a strong dosage of neo-liberal medicine (to be handed out by the West). Tony Blair would probably agree.

38 The Jordan, the Tiber and the Ganges, in: J. Hick and P. Knitter (eds.), *The Myth of Christian Uniqueness*, London: SCM, 1987, 89-116. I am using Panikkar's thoughts in the shape the educationalist John Hull has given them. Cp. John Hull, Christian

Christendom refers to the tradition's European phase, in which a geopolitical and social unity found itself squeezed between the unknown wastes of the Atlantic, the mysterious horror of Africa, and the threat of Islam to the East and South. *Christianity* is the universal and absolute system of belief accompanying Europe's expansion. It cancelled out other beliefs and to be Christian meant to agree to and believe certain things. Its identity was individualized and interiorised as "the fascinating verbalism of the name of God", including "a fetish-like numinosity of the isolated word", offering a non-mediated shortcut to God and, therefore, always in danger of spiritual self-deception.[39] There is no question that both forms of Christian faith are still around in both hemispheres. *Christianness* implies the attempt to go beyond the first two steps of the learning process by deconstructing the territorial and the cognitive boundaries of the tradition in the light of the situation confronting humanity today. This third phase is powered by a new spirituality focusing on a discipleship to Jesus and a Trinitarian epistemology. This approach does not waste Christian energies in the maintenance of boundaries between its own and other traditions, releasing them instead for the bigger project of God's love for the world through Jesus Christ. What Panikkar is describing here had a longer gestation period in the ecumenical movement. We must remember that already in the 1970s theologians predicted this theological departure leading to a new way of being Christian. One of these was the missiologist from Hamburg, Hans Jochen Margull who spoke of the future *Third-Worldliness* of Christianity. He had this to say:

> "Third-worldly means: in the situation of the tertia terra, the Third World. Concerning its definition a social-historical rather than a geographical interpretation is preferable. Therefore, third-worldly Christianity can be identified wherever (and therefore in non-Western Christianity in particular) Christ is believed to be on the side of the oppressed and Christian faith is understood authentically to be an act of comprehensive historical liberation."[40]

Boundaries, Christian Identities and the Local Church, in: *International Journal of Practical Theology* 1 (1999), 1-13.

39 Hull, 8f., 12.
40 Überseeische Christenheit II: Vermutungen zu einer Tertiaterranität des Christentums, in: *Verkündigung und Forschung* 19/1 (1974), 56-103; reprint (abridged) in Hans Jochen Margull, *Zeugnis und Dialog. Ausgewählte Schriften*, ed. by Theo Ahrens e.a.,

Margull continued by saying that part of the authenticity of any such third-worldly Christian experience, wherever it occurred, including the West, would be a confrontation with the paradigm of unity that much of western theology had upheld in the interest of its universal domination during the *Christianity* phase. The breaking of this unity through the rise of a new understanding of the Christian tradition is constitutive for the process of missionary transmission. This theological (not geographical) qualification of Third-Worldliness, or what has been dubbed Christianness, is very different from fundamentalism or a lack of theological sophistication.

Ammersbek bei Hamburg: Verlag an der Lottbek, 1992, 208-216. This edition was used here, quote on p. 211 f.

RELIGIOUS GLOBALIZATION AND WORLD CHRISTIANITY

Vinoth Ramachandra

Introduction

The twentieth century witnessed the greatest numerical growth of the Christian church in any century since the day of Pentecost. Today around one-third of the world's population adhere to some form of the Christian church, and this in the midst of some of the most aggressive persecutions of the church in recorded history. By 1900, the centrifugal centre in Roman Catholicism and Protestantism had moved from Europe to North America. North American churches, mission organizations, personnel, money and technology dominated the missionary movement throughout the twentieth century. By 2000, the centrifugal centre had moved southwards and eastwards. In China, for example, the growth of the church seems to be out of control, despite the ruthless attempts since the days of the Cultural Revolution to stamp it out. Though the strength of Chinese Christianity is in the villages, tens of thousands of academics, professionals and business people are meeting in small groups in urban areas to study the Bible. Chinese Christians are exploring ways to carry the Gospel to Southeast Asia and beyond, including by working in factories or going back to school in places like Vietnam, Cambodia or Myanmar. Will churches and missions from the South and East dominate the Christian movement in the twenty-first century?

Philip Jenkins, an American historian, is among those who think they will. His fascinating synthesis, *The Next Christendom: The Coming of Global Christianity*, contains little that is new to students of African, Latin American and Asian Christianity; but few have spelled out, as Jenkins does, the challenge this poses for the cultural empire of the liberal establishment of the North Atlantic. If American politicians, academics and the mass media want to understand the new world that is emerging, they need to pay far more attention than they have to 'the strangely unfamiliar world of the new Christianity'.[1]

---

1   Philip Jenkins, *The Next Christendom: The Coming of Global Christianity* (Oxford University Press, 2002) p.214

'Amazing as it may appear to a blasé West', writes Jenkins, 'Christianity exercises an overwhelming global appeal, which shows not the slightest sign of waning.'[2] His principal argument is that 'For the foreseeable future, the characteristic religious forms of Southern Christianity, enthusiastic and spontaneous, fundamentalistic and supernatural-oriented, look massively different from those of the older centres in Europe and North America.'[3] His trenchant marshalling of statistical and anecdotal evidence highlights the dilemmas that follow from the fact that if we are going to be non-judgmental (and 'politically correct') about the values and choices of others, then fellow Christians in the South cannot be denigrated for their spurning of liberal Western tutelage, not least on such issues as sexuality.

However, there is a strong 'Orientalising' tendency in Jenkins's book, given that his primary audience is the liberal academy and the mainstream churches of the USA: namely, to over-draw the distinctions between 'them' and 'us'. The 'them' are, for the most part, vigorously growing Pentecostal and independent Southern churches, 'enthusiastic and spontaneous, fundamentalistic and supernatural-oriented', while the 'us' are rational, sober, liberal, mainstream Christians inhabiting declining churches in the North. Interestingly, whenever he wants to illustrate for Northern audiences the political courage (sometimes culminating in martyrdom at the hands of ruthless dictators) of Southern Christian leaders, the examples he gives are always drawn from Roman Catholic and Protestant churches.

Furthermore, Jenkins highlights the 'folk religious' character of southern Christianity, with its vision of a world suffused with spiritual powers that impinge on human life. Jenkins writes: 'If there is a single key area of faith and practice that divides Northern and Southern Christians, it is this matter of spiritual forces and their effects on the everyday human world. The issue goes to the heart of cultural definition and worldviews.'[4] But this is to underplay the role that similar beliefs and practices play among many Northerners, including the many flourishing charismatic/Pentecostal churches in American and European cities. Moreover, walk into any major 'secular' bookstore in any city in the North and you will find that works on

---

2 Ibid.p.39
3 Ibid.p.78
4 Ibid.p.123

mainstream Christianity and Enlightenment philosophy are massively outnumbered by books and cassettes on astrology, magic, shamanism, witchcraft, faith-healing and other exotic phenomena. Is this really a difference of Southern and Northern worldviews? Aren't there profound differences that cut right across the simple binary opposition of North/South? After all, the Harry Potter phenomenon did not originate among the hill-tribes of Thailand.

A related tendency is to blur important differences between grass-roots initiated, pre-modern churches and what has come to be called Neo-Pentecostal churches. Unlike the former, the latter tend to concentrate in cities and take a strongly negative stance towards traditional cultural and religious customs. The richer churches among them lean towards an 'Americanization' of church practice, with pastors and evangelists imitating the styles of flamboyant American tele-evangelists. Indeed, apart from language, there is little to distinguish typical Neo-Pentecostal worship services in London, Sao Paulo, Nairobi or Singapore. This is not to disparage, but rather to understand the interplay of local and global forces. Deeply disturbing though the abuses of power and exploitation of peoples' gullibility are, too many people have experienced healing in their lives for us not to take the healing practices of these churches seriously. Also, on the social level, many of the new churches among the poor have provided sites of resistance where peoples' humanity has been reaffirmed in contexts which continually deny it.

Jenkins glides over the influence that rich Northern churches have on many pastors in Africa and Latin America, especially via television and the new global communications media. He points out that as economic circumstances have deteriorated, many are led to a life in the church, as one of the few opportunities available. Prosperity gospels, however, did not arise from among the poor and seem to be in conflict with the immediate experience of most Southern Christians. Their popularity may well illustrate one of the processes widely recognized as characteristic of the postmodern global condition. As Bernice Martin observes, from a Central American context, they 'display a direct connection between the local and the global which leapfrogs over the national level, and is greatly assisted in doing so by (post)modern communications.' She adds:

'There is little doubt that an important source of pride and validation among many of the new Protestants is a sense of being part of a worldwide movement of *winners*, however humble and obscure their particular group may seem. This has both a theological dimension, which can include a sense of shared genealogy with the Reformation theologians of northern Europe, and a broader geopolitical dimension, which involves a consciousness of being on the same side as the biggest and most successful players in the global development game, notably, though not exclusively, the USA. As one Mexican Bible translator put it: "We have been held back by Catholicism far too long on this continent."[5]

Observations such as these problematize the popular notion of 'indigeneity'. Moreover, postcolonial writers such as Gayatri Spivak have questioned the naive assumption that we can easily recover 'indigenous' traditions and voices untainted by the colonial experience. In my view, many of the examples given in missiology texts of 'indigenous Christian movements' in South and South-East Asia are in fact movements heavily influenced theologically by certain Western (usually US) forms of Christianity. It is likely that, given the dominance of US material resources in global mission, that these trends will continue well into the twenty-first century, even as the vast majority of cross-cultural missionaries will be non-Western.

It seems, then, that Jenkins' exposure to Southern Christianity is as limited as his exposure to Northern Christianity. He underplays the degree of theological diversity and disagreement in the South. He tends to identify every anti-Western critique that emanates from the Southern church as 'fundamentalist'; so, he does a great disservice to Southern Christianity by simplifying its complexity and distorting its story.

If Jenkins' principal subject is the southward shift of Christianity, his second is the encounter of Christianity and Islam as they expand through migration and missionary outreach all the way from West Africa to Irian Jaya. And here too there is a significant downplaying of both the global geopolitical realities and the differing local political contexts that shape the encounter of such major faiths. 'At the turn of the third millennium', he writes, 'religious loyalties are at the root of many of the world's ongoing civil wars and political violence, and in

5   Bernice Martin, 'From Pre-to Postmodernity in Latin America: The Case of Pentecostalism' in Paul Heelas (ed) *Religion, Modernity and Postmodernity* (Oxford: Blackwells, 1998) p.123

many cases, the critical division is the age-old battle between Christianity and Islam.'[6] We are informed that 'the critical political frontiers around the world are not decided by attitudes toward class or dialectical materialism, but by rival concepts of God.'[7] Not surprisingly, a long discussion on the tragedy in the Sudan makes no mention of the influence of either oil or ethnic (as opposed to religious) identities on the disintegration of that country. Nor are the interesting connections noted between, say, the popularity of Islam among black groups in the US contesting the cultural hegemony of white colonial Christianity and the popularity of Pentecostalism in traditional Roman Catholic societies in south and central America.

We need a more nuanced understanding of religious trans-formations and of 'religious conflict' if we are to respond to these with Christian integrity. If it is 'rival concepts of God' that decide 'political frontiers around the world', why have the most bitter wars in history (and right up to the present day) been waged between co-religionists and not between adherents of rival religious loyalties? As Fred Halliday of the London School of Economics observes, 'Islam may, in some contexts, be the prime form of political and social identity, but it is never the sole form and is often not the primary one. Within Muslim societies divisions of ethnicity matter much, often more than a shared religious identity; this is equally so in emigration... No one can understand the politics of, say, Turkey, Pakistan or Indonesia on the basis of Islam alone. Despite rhetoric, Islam explains little of what happens in these societies.'[8]

Wherever we live in the new millennium, in the North no less than in the South, we shall increasingly encounter new religious movements and also communities staking political claims in the name of ancient religious identities and traditions. It is imperative, therefore, that we pay close attention to these transformations as they bring fresh challenges to the church's witness. This is especially, but certainly by no means exclusively, the case in relation to Muslim peoples. I argue that we need to contest those images (in academic circles no less than the popular media) of a resurgent, global 'Islam', conceived as a bloc universe, as much as we should gratefully receive- but move beyond -

6   Jenkins,op.cit., p.163
7   Ibid.
8   Fred Halliday, *Two Hours That Shook the World: Sept 11 2001: Causes and Consequences* (London: Saqi Books, 2002) p.126

Jenkins' work and challenge the stereotypes of a monolithic 'Christianity' in the South.

False Antitheses

Throughout history, Muslims and Christians have traded, studied and negotiated with each other across the frontiers of religious differences. The neat civilizational blocs imagined by writers such as Bernard Lewis or Samuel Huntington have always been more porous than the mere textual study of religions suggests. One fascinating example that the Palestinian scholar, Nabil Matar, gives in his book *Turks, Moors, and Englishmen in the Age of Discovery*[9] is the following. In 1603, Ahmad-al-Mansur, the King of Morocco, presented his English ally, Queen Elizabeth I, with a simple proposal: England would help the Moors colonize America. The King proposed that Moroccan and English troops, using English ships, should attack the Spanish colonies in America, expel their hated Spanish enemies, and then 'possesse' the land and keep it 'under our dominion for ever, and - by the help of God - to joyne it to our estate and yours.' There was a catch, however. Might it not be more sensible, suggested the King, that most of the future colonists should be Moroccan rather than English? For 'in respect of the great heat of the clymat, where those of your countrie doe not fynde themselfes fitt to endure the extremetie of heat there and of the cold of your partes, where our men endure it very well by reason that the heat hurtes them not.'[10] After due consideration, the Moroccan offer was not taken up by Her Majesty.

But what is noteworthy is that such a proposal raised few eyebrows at the time. After all, the English were close allies of both the Moroccans and their Ottoman overlords. Rivalry among Christians was always a powerful factor leading to alliances and arrangements between Muslims and Christian states. The English might have their reservations about Islam, but these were nothing compared to their hatred and fear of 'Popery'. As well as treaties of trade and friendship this alliance led to several joint expeditions, such as an Anglo-Moroccan attack on Cadiz in 1596. It also led to a great movement of people between the two worlds, as Matar's work points out. Elizabethan London had a burgeoning Muslim community, which

---

9   New York: Columbia University Press, 1999
10   Ibid.p.9

encompassed a large party of Turkish ex-prisoners, some Moorish craftsmen, and a number of wealthy Turkish merchants.[11]

Historians such as Christopher Bayly have noted that the nineteenth-century was a period not of widespread religious scepticism but of multi-centred religious ferment.[12] Religion, secularism and nationalism interpenetrated each other all over the world, creating permutations and hybrids of dizzying variety. Islam, Hinduism and Buddhism began to re-configure themselves as 'world religions' in response to Christian evangelism, but also in the wake of the new possibilities brought about by printing and communication. They borrowed extensively from European thought but also drew deeply on their own theological and cultural traditions. Hindu religious texts could now be standardized, printed and disseminated as never before. Pilgrimage to Mecca became more practicable and affordable, and Muslims from all over the world could now sit at the feet of the great Muslim teachers of the Middle East, thus stimulating a greater uniformity and a sense of global Islamic brotherhood. The rash of nineteenth-century church-building in Britain was matched by the construction of temples, mosques and other places of non-Christian worship across Africa and Asia. And, goaded by the vigorous assertion and renewal of non-European religions, Christianity was in turn forced to rethink its own identity.

Moreover, '[I]t was religion', writes Linda Colley in her study of the formation of 'Great Britain' from 1707 onwards, 'that first converted peasants into patriots, long before the onset of modernisation in the shape of railroads, mass education, advanced press networks and democracy.'[13] The impact of Protestant Christianity on the development of British national identity, however, tends to be ignored in contemporary political theory. Liberal theorists take it for granted that religious discourse is antithetical to both liberty and the rationality of the public square. Religious conviction was a major source of the moral indignation and political debate that surrounded the abolitionist movements or the national soul-searching over the operations of the British East India Company (climaxing in Edmund Burke's searing indictment of Warren Hastings in the parliamentary debates of 1787).

---

11 Cf. Nabil Matar, *Islam in Britain, 1558-1685* (Cambridge University Press, 2001)
12 C.A. Bayly, *The Birth of the Modern World, 1780-1914* (Oxford: Blackwells, 2004) Ch.9
13 Linda Colley, *Britons: Forging the Nation 1707-1837* (New Haven and London: Yale University Press, 1992) p.369

The agitations for and against Catholic emancipation, the evangelical anti-slavery petitions and campaigns, the emergence of Bible societies and voluntary missionary associations: these all were crucial to the creation of a public sphere and national identity.

Their counterparts in nineteenth-century India were the anti-*sati* Hindu reform movements, the Ramakrishna missions, and the cow protection campaigns of the Arya Samaj. Ironically, the demand by Christian churches and missionary agencies for the colonial state not to support non-Christian places of worship led to the formation of a public sphere in which religious movements produced an anti-colonial 'Hindu spirituality' that was fully modern.[14] The separation of church and state does not lead to the decline of the social and political importance of religion. Even as Protestant Christianity came to be linked increasingly with British and American cultural identities, so did Brahmanical Hinduism with Indian nationalism and Theravada Buddhism with Ceylonese nationalism. With the rise of the nation-state the meaning of religion is also transformed.

Religious Globalizations[15]

In the modern nation-state all who live within a particular territory are defined as constituting a 'nation' and of being 'citizens' of a political community. To be a citizen is to abstract away one's ethnic, religious and other particularities, and to act as a member of the political community. The state expects all its citizens to subscribe to an identical way of defining themselves and relating to each other and to the state. Modern states, including liberal democracies, are suspicious of, and feel threatened by, well-organized ethnic, religious and other communities lest these become rival centres of loyalty.

We have seen that religion has been, and continues to be, an important resource for nationalist, modernizing movements. The rise of religious renewal movements has served to question the legitimacy of the secular nation-state. Moreover, globalizing processes both corrode inherited cultural and personal identities and, at the same time, stimulate the revitalisation of particular identities as a way of gaining

---

14 Cf. Peter van der Veer, *Imperial Encounters: Religion and Modernity in India and Britain* (Princeton University Press, 2001)

15 Much of the material that follows in this essay overlaps with my Alexander Duff Mission Lecture, given at New College, Edinburgh and the International Christian College, Glasgow, in May 2005.

more power or influence in this new global order. What was true of Protestant Christianity in the world of Victorian Britain also applies to the nationalist transformations of Hindu Neo-Vedanta, Theravada Buddhism, Shintoism and Shi'ite Islam in the non-Western world. Religions are not unchanging, ahistorical 'essences', and we cannot understand them or their adherents apart from their historical, political and social contexts.

Religious nationalism (Hindu, Muslim, Buddhist, Christian) assumes different forms in different societies; but in all societies it has one overriding goal. The common enemy is the secular state, and the goal is not so much to convert other people to their beliefs, as to seize power, political and social, within their own societies. The postcolonial secular state, which most countries have adopted after independence from the European colonial powers, has proved to be inefficient, biased and corrupt, unable to deliver its promises of freedom and prosperity. Islamism is a form of protest – political and discursive – within these societies against social and political power that excludes them from power. As Mawlana Mawdudi (1903-1979), founder of the Jamaat-I-Islami party in Pakistan and whose influence on Islamist movements worldwide has been considerable, once said: 'In human affairs the most important thing is, "who holds the bridle reigns?" If these are in the hands of righteous people, worshippers of God, then it is inevitable that the whole of social life be God-worshipping... None of the purposes of religion can be accomplished so long as control of affairs is in the hands of *kafirs*.'[16]

Religious nationalisms thus represent not a throwback to a medieval past, but rather a thoroughly contemporary, modern phenomenon. Fred Halliday writes about the 1979 Iranian revolution as follows: 'For all the appearance that Iran underwent a return to the past and that its revolution was "traditional", it was in some respects modern, indeed perhaps the most modern social revolution seen in any country. It took place not among the peasantry, but among the urban poor and middle classes, and it achieved its aims not in the main through violence, but through political means, the mass opposition protest and the political general strike. The paradox of the Iranian

---

16 Quoted in T.N. Madan, *Modern Myths, Locked Minds: Secularism and Fundamentalism in India* (Delhi: Oxford University Press, 1998) p.141

revolution was that it was both the most traditional and the most modern of social revolutions.'[17]

Consider, as another well-known instance, the rise of Hindutva in India. Traditional India had a very weak concept of a centralizing state, but Hindu nationalists want a strong central state to unite the Hindus of the country, along with nuclear weapons and foreign investment to make India a global superpower on the world stage. It sees *shakti*, or power, as the currency of the world and believes that India has for centuries lacked this because of its domination by Muslim and other foreign powers. It must now learn the lessons of its history and acquire *shakti* in its military, economic and political forms. Globalisation becomes crucial, not so much to gain access to other cultures as to bring in foreign capital and accelerate the rate of economic growth, measure up to China, and get locked into the emerging global economic and political order.

The Indian and Chinese diasporas today are significant carriers of cultural and religious globalization, especially as professionals and business entrepreneurs have replaced the cheap migrant labour of the nineteenth and early twentieth centuries. Moreover, the movement of modern forms of Hinduism and Buddhism around the world through the efforts of travelling gurus and monks is an important event in recent times that has taken place alongside the emigration of South Asians and South Asian culture. The re-launching of Hindu Vedanta, first by Vivekananda in the 1890s and then by the innumerable gurus who have followed in his wake, as a 'global spirituality' (in contrast to what is taken to be the narrow historical particularism of the Christian faith) continues to resonate among the affluent classes of our postmodern world. Vedanta's central notion of spiritual hierarchy and levels of truth enables it to encompass all religions without leaving any doubt as to its own superiority.

The New Age movement represents the colonisation and commercialisation of Indian religious traditions – bits and pieces from yoga, Indian erotic art, meditation techniques, Ayurvedic massage, and such like are cobbled together and sold back to Indian middle-classes. One scholar has dubbed this process of re-enculturation the 'Pizza

---

17 Halliday, op.cit. p.62

36

Effect'.[18]   The original pizza was a Neapolitan bread which was exported to America from Italy, embellished, and returned to Italy where it became a national dish. The Hindutva movement, drawing its support from Indian immigrants in the West and the urban middle-classes in India, has built on Orientalist understandings of Indian religions and presented a 'Global Hinduism' through the mirror of the West.

Cosmopolitan Islam v Islamism

In Muslim-majority countries there has raged an intellectual and political battle among Muslim thinkers and activists to reinterpret the Qur'an and the prophetic traditions in the light of modern challenges. The backdrop is the humiliating experience of Western political, cultural and intellectual domination since the early nineteenth century. Among the modern educated classes, a new style of Muslim intellectual has emerged, committed to the transformation of society but within the framework of ideologies and programs that could be identified as authentically Islamic.

In advocating the rejection of secular, individualistic values which have accompanied the modernization process in the West, the new Islamists thus provided an important focus for marginalized, excluded and alienated social groups. Students have often been the target of repressive governments, such as in Indonesia under General Suharto. They were critical of the failures of development, corruption, the growing disparity between rich and poor, and conspicuous consumption in a society with limited opportunities for the younger generation. When student organizations were banned in universities, mosques became rallying centres for disaffected students. Islamic discourse, often initiated by Muslim intellectuals educated in Europe and the Middle East, now became the chief vehicle to express dissent. With the political door closed, the stress was now placed on the relevance of Islam to social and economic development.

The current struggle in Indonesia, the world's most populous Muslim nation, is instructive for what is happening elsewhere. Indonesia boasts a rich pluralist heritage, especially in Java where ancient Hindu, Buddhist and animist traditions have coalesced and created a uniquely Javanese worldview and tolerant culture. In large measure, the ideological battle now being waged is a clash of two

---

18   Gavin Flood, *An Introduction to Hinduism* (Cambridge: Cambridge University Press, 1996) p.267

cultures: between this indigenous, pluralist Islam (what some writers call 'cosmopolitan Islam') and the legalistic, Arabic Islam propagated by proselytizing movements from Saudi Arabia and Egypt.

Cosmopolitan Islam is more concerned with political culture than political institutions. It is expressed in the individual lives and morality of the people, informing the social ethics of the community and its sense of a transnational or universal identity. Many local Muslim intellectuals, as well as broad segments of the public, endorse a pluralist understanding of nationhood. 'Civil pluralist Muslims', writes the scholar Robert Hefner, 'deny the necessity of a formally established Islamic state, emphasize that it is the spirit and not the letter of Islamic law (*shariah*) to which Muslims must attend, stress the need for programmes to elevate the status of women, and insist that the Muslim world's most urgent task is to develop moral tools to respond to the challenge of modern pluralism.'[19]

However, the spread of global communications, the radicalization of some Islamist groups, and the rise of a free-floating transnational army of fighters ('jihadis') drawing their support from Pakistan, the Arab world, south-east Asia and Chechnya, has meant that conflict in one part of the Muslim world, with its specific local causes and character, is immediately presented and utilized as part of conflict in another region. The globalization of local conflicts serves powerful propaganda purposes. However, it would be a gross distortion to identify the global transformations of Islam, and indeed of other world religions, that are taking place today with their more violent and fanatical forms. The latter command more media-footage, that's all.

Global Christian Integrity

The Church is a truly global community, and largely a church *of* the poor. Furthermore, 'What at first glance appears to be the largest world religion,' writes Dana Roberts, 'is in fact the ultimate local religion. Indigenous words for God and ancient forms of spirituality have all become part of Christianity. Flexibility at the local level, combined with being part of an international network, is a major factor

---

19 Robert W. Hefner, 'Secularization and Citizenship in Modern Indonesia' in Paul Heelas (ed.) *Religion, Modernity and Postmodernism* (Oxford: Blackwells, 1998) p.148. For a large-scale survey of widely divergent attitudes in four Muslim-majority countries, including Indonesia, see Riaz Hassan, *Faithlines: Muslim Conceptions of Islam and Society* (Oxford University Press, 2001)

in Christianity's self-understanding and success today. The strength of world Christianity lies in its creative interweaving of the warp of a world religion with the woof of its local contexts.'[20]

If our global Christian witness in the political arena is to carry integrity, I suggest the following personal and collective responses, wherever we may happen to live:

1. Take the trouble to learn the history behind the stories of 'religious violence' reported in the secular media. 'Religious Violence' is a notoriously difficult concept. It works within a modern secularist worldview that draws neat categorical distinctions between 'religion', 'politics', 'culture', and so on. In most Asian societies, 'religious' conversion has always been seen as a political act, a re-distribution of political identities and loyalties. It was central to the debates in pre-independence India and the religious categories used to classify people in official censuses were strongly contested right up to the drawing up of the Constitution in 1951. (The same ambivalence is found in post-Reformation Britain, say, right until the mid-nineteenth century. Locke's famous treatise on religious toleration excludes Roman Catholics from the purview of toleration because they are seen as fundamentally a political community whose final loyalties lie elsewhere). In non-European contexts, where religious identities are still strong, all modernizing as well as counter-modernizing movements express themselves in religious terminology.

The causes of 'religious violence' - whether directed by one 'religious group' against the state or against another 'religious group', or by a 'religious state' against national minorities - vary enormously from one context to another, even within Asia, that we dare not make facile generalizations. Often the precipitating factors have little to do with religious beliefs or practices, but once conflict arises religion is quickly invoked by both parties as a way of drawing in support from co-religionists elsewhere. Moreover, it is minority Muslim groups (such as the Shiites and Ahmadiyyas) in Islamic states who have borne the brunt of Islamist violence, not Western states, Western tourists or local Christian populations. The deep differences that run through, as well as between, Muslim-majority states are sometimes obscured by pan-Islamic rhetoric.

---

20   Dana L. Robert, 'Shifting Southward: Global Christianity Since 1945', *International Bulletin of Missionary Research*, vol.24.no.2, April 2000, p.56

Nothing does more to unite the fractious Islamic world, or to turn it against its Christian minorities, than a US attack on one or another prostrate Muslim state. The US invasions of Afghanistan and Iraq are exactly the sort of adventure that Christians in Muslim-majority nations have learned to dread, and it is they who suffer for what is seen as the aggression of the West.

Many minority groups are overwhelmed or dominated by majority (or dominant) ethnic groups in Asia and Africa. Christian conversion gives them a sense of dignity and self-worth and empowers them to break free from subordination. This is how one Indian Christian historian describes the social and political effects of conversion and the reasons for the consequent persecution of Christian *dalits* and tribal peoples (*adivasis*) in his country:

'[T]he new Christians give up alcoholic consumption, gambling, and many such social vices. They weigh their agricultural products before taking them to the market so that the buyers cannot cheat them. They also do not spend money lavishly on religious festivals. They do not go to the village medicine men or exorcists to get rid of their sickness. Moreover, the new Christians do not borrow money from moneylenders, and as a result the economic income of the local toddy-sellers, agricultural traders, grocery merchants, religious priests, medicine men and moneylenders decreases. Once Christians are able to read and write, they become familiar with their rights and responsibilities, and are no longer willing to undertake menial jobs without appropriate compensation. Their regained human dignity and respect beckon them to live as human beings. This also results in confrontation with the millennia-old traditions of suppression and exploitation. The new consciousness of *Adivasis*, *Dalits* and tribal people questions the legitimacy of the religious and social foundations that are laid and protected by the people of the sanskritic religions. The social and economic consequences of the conversion of the *Adivasis*, *Dalits* and tribal people to Christianity have been the immediate reason for violent reactions of the followers of the Hindutva.'[21]

2. Identify and build relationships with the more moderate, self-critical voices within the other religious traditions and communities among whom we live. It is this kind of dialogue, born of

---

21   Daniel Jeyaraj, 'Christian Missions in the Context of Hindutva- A Personal Reflection', *Dharma Deepika*, July-Dec 2004, p.48

personal friendships, that will help us avoid simplistic generalizations and stereotyping of other religious cultures and traditions. And if Muslims rightly resent the negative stereotyping of a monolithic Islam by Western writers, then they need to look with equal dismay at the identical stereotyping that is widespread in the Muslim world. Anti-Western polemic often blends with anti-Christian sentiments, even in the more serious Muslim literature. Moreover, Kate Zebiri, a lecturer in Arabic and Islamic Studies at the University of London, has noted that 'the study of Christianity by modern Muslims does not, on the whole, compare favourably with that of the medieval scholars', many of whom considered it important to understand the arguments and doctrines of Christianity on their own terms before seeking to refute them.[22] Ironically, 'Christianity is sometimes portrayed in the very same terms that have been used of Islam in both earlier orientalist scholarship and the contemporary media: as power-seeking and war-mongering on the one hand, and irrational, obscurantist, backward-looking, and in need of reformation on the other.'[23]

All phobias are the result of ignorance and the inability to look critically at oneself and one's own community. Good relations can only be established between Christians and Muslims in the West if Christians were forthright in exposing and condemning all expressions of anti-Muslim bigotry in the West, and if Muslim leaders were to, with equal fervour, condemn similar bigotry and discrimination by their own ranks both in the West and in what they regard as the *dar-ul-Islam*. Across Europe it seems that a new generation of Muslims is becoming active in democratic politics. In this media-dominated age, may the nature of Muslim-Christian relations in cities like Birmingham or Marseilles be crucial for Muslim-Christian relations elsewhere in the world?

3. We need to engage actively in the political quest for truly participatory democracies that honour cultural and religious differences. In a hegemonic secular culture, as in the liberal democracies of the West, authentic cross-cultural engagement is stifled or circumvented. In the name of the liberal-procedural state, or the alleged neutral objectivity of Western science, other ways of life are, at best, reduced to exotic commodities for tourist consumption. They are not allowed to challenge the prevailing political paradigm.

---

22 Kate Zebiri, *Muslims and Christians Face to Face* (Oxford: Oneworld, 1997) p.173
23 Ibid. p.174

There is a militant secularist 'orthodoxy' that is as destructive of authentic pluralism as its fundamentalist religious counterpart. This is seen, for instance, in the French government's ruling against the wearing of the *hijab* by Muslim schoolgirls, or the hysterical vilification in the mass media of any public figure who rejects the liberal rhetoric of 'reproductive rights' or 'sexual preferences'. Secularization is not an inevitable process thrown up by abstract, impersonal forces that are subsumed under the label of 'modernity'. It is often actively promoted by vested interests (whether academics, artists, businessmen or journalists). Intellectuals are especially prone to see themselves as romantic heroes, representing the mythical cult of 'originality', i.e., the unique, that which emerges from the genius of the individual who is free from all the constrictions of tradition, community, conventions and obligations.

For Christians, the relationship of church and state has to be framed in terms of the eschatological reign of Christ, not of the empirical Church or Christianity. What form this relationship assumes will surely depend on historical and cultural context.[24] A secularism that rejects the Christendom ideal need not fall prey to the equally mythical notion of an ideologically neutral state. Indian Christians, for instance, have unanimously supported the Indian conception of secularism that is not a replication of the American or the French model, worked out under her own historical conditions. Can we imagine a spectrum of *contextual secularisms*, each arising from a 'grass roots' dialogue, negotiation, and compromise; not imposed from the 'top down' by a Western-educated secularized elite?

What would emerge from such an enterprise could be a context-specific charter of rights and duties, designed to protect the integrity and freedoms of human persons. The Christian strategy in this dialogue would be to appeal to reasons *internal* to the faith traditions of other communities, and not only explicitly Christian arguments, to press for legislation and public policy that Christians believe would enhance human flourishing. Would it not be possible, say, for Christians to encourage Islamists to see that traditional interpretations of *shar'ia* may actually contradict Quranic teaching, or that the worship of Allah must be uncoerced if it is to be authentic? Or to show people of all faiths that

---

24 For the following argument see my *Faiths in Conflict?: Christian Integrity in a Multicultural World* (Leicester, UK: Inter-Varsity Press, 1999) pp. 160-2

any religion that requires state patronage for its survival loses its moral authority and becomes vulnerable to corruption?

The answer to the 'naked public square', then, is not a 'sacred public square' envisaged by religious nationalists (whether Muslim, Hindu, Buddhist or Christian), but a *civic* public square: a place of public moral discourse, which discourse must of necessity draw on the resources of the various religious communities that comprise the polity. We all agree that a morally and culturally 'neutral' state which makes no moral demands on its citizens and is equally hospitable to all cultures and conceptions of the good is logically incoherent and practically impossible. And since every law coerces those not sharing its underlying values, a morally and culturally non-coercive state is a fantasy. Openly recognizing this fact is the first step forward in reconfiguring the nature of politics. Christians should not respond by demanding a state that renders no metaphysical or religious judgments (for this is an impossibility) but rather by demanding a state that renders these judgments more openly, precisely so that they can be subjected to public scrutiny and debate.

Africa has seen a greater involvement by church leaders in political life compared to Asia, but they have often lacked a clearly Christian social agenda. Indeed, some of the most terrible atrocities in Africa in recent times have been committed in nations (such as Liberia and Rwanda) where the collusion between church and state has been overt. Some writers, including Jenkins, have suggested that we may see a reversion to older models of Christendom in some parts of Africa. It is doubtful if we shall see a return to the organicism of church and society that characterised medieval Europe, but, under the perceived threat of Islam, some African countries will be tempted to mobilize their identities in Christian terms. If the Christian-majority nations of Africa are not to repeat the betrayals of the Gospel that characterised European Christendom, then they must develop a vision of a *multiculturally constituted*, shared political culture. Diverse identities in national life are not a threat to our own identity, but, rather, are indispensable for the discovery of our own distinctiveness in reciprocal relatedness to our neighbour.

Christians in Western nations are now in a position to rediscover what is authentically Christian, and to engage with secularism and new religious movements with integrity, humility and courage. Alexis de

Tocqueville, that astute commentator on the American experiment in democracy, warned against a 'democratic despotism', meaning not crude majoritarian rule but an apathetic majority supinely surrendering power to elite minorities. This seems to be where Europe and the USA are headed. Is it fanciful to suppose that the situation of Christians - and others who adhere to religious faiths that assert strong truth claims and make strong demands on their members - will come to resemble *dhimmitude*, the status of non-Muslims in a number of Islamic countries? The *dhimmi* is tolerated so long as his beliefs are confined to his religious community and his public acts do not offend the state ideology.

As Oliver O'Donovan has perceived, the 'ambiguities' of Christendom 'arose from a loss of focus on its missionary context'. 'The peril of the Christendom idea- precisely the same peril that attends upon the post-Christendom idea of the religiously neutral state- was that of negative collusion: the pretence that there was now no further challenge to be issued to the rulers in the name of the ruling Christ.' O'Donovan continues: 'The church does not philosophise about a future world; it demonstrates the working of the coming Kingdom within this one. Through the authorisation of the Holy Spirit it squares up to civil authority and confronts it. This may lead to martyrdom, or to mutual service.'[25]

So we may well be seeing a convergence of Christian experience globally, with Western Christians learning what their brethren in most parts of the world have been experiencing, to varying degrees, for centuries: to live on terms set by other people. But this oppressive situation is also, from another perspective, the *essential missionary experience*: i.e., being vulnerable and dependent on others; entering 'alien worlds' and responding to the issues and questions of importance to their inhabitants, rather than expecting them to enter 'our world' and learn our theological language; raising disturbing questions from within other worldviews that would profoundly re-orient their cultures and societies, while in turn being compelled to rethink our own understandings of Bible and theology. This missionary situation was the first learning experience that European Christianity received from its contact with the non-Western world.

---

25 Oliver O'Donovan, *The Desire of the Nations: Rediscovering the Roots of Political Theology* (Cambridge University Press, 1996) pp.212-3, 217

Much of the credibility of global Christianity in the present millennium will depend on whether Christians (whether in Europe, Asia or North America) can resist the identities imposed on them by their nation-state and/or their ethnic communities, and grasp that their primary allegiance is to Jesus Christ and his universal reign. Recovering the visible unity of the global church is more important at the present time (when a false universalism masquerades as globalization) than celebrations of cultural diversity. This is a special challenge today when Christian mission is no longer mono-cultural, mono-denominational, or mono-directional. Most Christians, north and south, have lost the conviction - that was so central to the teaching of Jesus and the apostles, and recovered in the early days of the ecumenical movement- that the unity (inclusive of diversity) of the church is at the heart of the Gospel itself. Any concept of mission that ignores that fact is simply a mission other than the *missio Dei*.

GLOBAL CHRISTIANITY IS CHANGING.
HOW DO THESE CHANGES INFLUENCE CONFLICT AND PEACE?

Viggo Mortensen

Recently I was standing in the Hagia Sofia in Istanbul. Although the building is in a bad shape and in need of restoration (that also is constantly going on but at a slow pace) one is struck by awe and admiration. The building goes back to 537 when the emperor Justinian thought he had beaten King Solomon in erecting this temple in what should be the new Rome. The cupola spans 31 x 33 metres, 56 metres above the floor. When my forefathers, the Vikings, a couple of hundred years later, came down in their small boats from their one storey wooden structures in the cold North they must have been flabbergasted. This edifice bears witness to the fact that it is the product of a society that puts its enormous technological skill in the service of a vision for Christian spirituality and ecclesial power. A *monument for global Christianity if ever there was one.*

Today - after a tumultuous history, half of its time church, half of its time mosque – the place is a museum, and there are no (or very few) local Christians in sight; officially 99% of all inhabitants of present day Turkey are Moslems. Thus the Hagia Sofia bears witness to the fact that Christianity is a religion on the move. Because a certain region and people have accepted the Gospel, it is not at all sure that it will stay Christian. As the Seer noticed: The lampstands can be removed (Rev. 2:4). Christianity is a historic religion. Normally we would consider this a strength. Christianity has a beginning. Does it also have an end?

The next Christendom

It is difficult to predict, - especially the future, a Danish saying goes. That is also the case when it comes to the future of Christianity. Reviewing statements from academics and social commentators about the future of Christianity one is torn between pessimism and optimism. Only one thing seems clear: the scene is changing and changing fast and there is little sense of direction.

In my contribution to a recent book[1] I argue that we in Western Europe are going through a period of religious change. The British sociologist of religion Grace Davie is saying the same when she states: "The "keystone" of the arch of European values is crumbling...Europe is in the process of removing the "keystone" in the arch of its value system, without being altogether clear about what should be put in its place".[2]

The same claim can be substantiated by the analysis of Philip Jenkins.[3] In view of the demographic changes that will be happening, Jenkins describes how the future Christendom will probably look like. By the year 2050, at least six nations, i.e., Brazil, Mexico, the Philippines, Nigeria, Congo and the US will have more than 100 millions of Christians. Africa south of Sahara will long before have overtaken Europe in the number of Christians. Brazil will have 150 millions of Catholics and 40 million of Protestants. And more than a billion of Pentecostals will spread their version of Christianity.

In the southern hemisphere we will see a wave of non-democratic states with theocratic tendencies, which will compete for regional superiority. If these Christians can manage not to fight between themselves, they will gang up against the common enemy, Islam. 20 out of the 25 largest states will either be Christian or Islamic and at least 10 will be the scenes of bloody conflicts. Even though there may be a nominal majority of Christians, Islam will have the upper hand in these third-world wars, often supported by the industrialized states in the North, which, because of the harsh economic facts, will tone down their emotional preference for Christianity. Extremists within both religions will still make sure that women's rights, freedom of religion and other wild ideas of the secularised North will not gain ground. At the same time, leading countries in Africa and Asia are developing a considerable military potential. These prospects for the future might very well make the 16th century's deadly religious wars look like a Sunday school excursion.

1   *For All God's People: Being Church in Multireligious Societies.* In Viggo Mortensen (ed.) *Theology and the Religions: A Dialogue,* (Grand Rapids: Wm. B. Eerdmanns, 2003) p.465-479
2   Grace Davie: *Europe: The Exceptional Case.*(Sarum Theological lectures: London 2002) p.147
3   Philip Jenkins: *The Next Christendom. The Coming of Global Christianity.* (Oxford University Press 2002)

Philip Jenkins considers this prospect of the future to be due to the Third World's demographic explosion, the poor slum dwellers' hope of rescue and the Muslim-Christians competition for souls and proselytising work. Jenkins would not hesitate to say that these predictions might *not* come true. On the other hand, like most futurologists, he extrapolates on the basis of the present tendencies.[4]

What are these tendencies? In short: Christianity has become global and it is undergoing transformation.

Christianity on the move

Christianity is a religion that is not bound in time and space. It is a religion made to travel. History documents it. Whereas Christianity was the prevalent religion in Europe and America until about a hundred years ago, the 19th and 20th centuries have seen the revolutionary change that Christianity has become global. The reason for this is the activities of the Christian missionary movements. The slogan was, as at the famous World Missionary Conference at Edinburgh in 1910: Christianisation of the world in this generation. Looking at the figures, we must admit that this has not been the case. The world is not Christian. Christianity has increased, but less than the growth of the population. The Christian missionary movement, however, called forward the religions. The missionaries set out to find and convert "pagans", but they found people belonging to another faith. This religious encounter, which grew out of the missionary movement, radically transformed not only the indigenous cultures but also Christianity; that now became one of all the world's religions. It became itself a global religion.

Having won the Jewish-Roman war in the year 70, the Roman emperor Titus, in proof of having conquered Jerusalem with the Jewish temple, took the seven branched candlestick, the Menorah, and brought it back to Rome in triumph. How this happened can still be seen at the Arch of Titus. We all know about the disastrous and far-reaching consequences of this for the Jewish people, who since then have constructed an identity as a people living in diaspora. But, in a way, it

---

4   "Such extrapolations of the present, whether retrospective or predictive, are potentially dangerous and misleading. But they are also interesting – which is presumably why so many people do it."
     Alister E. McGrath: *The Future of Christianity*. (Blackwell Manifestos: Oxford 2002) p.72

affected the first Christians just as much. As we learn in the first chapters of the Acts of the Apostles, they lived as a Jewish sect, whose lives centred around the cult in the temple of Jerusalem. "Every day they continued to meet together in the temple courts" (Acts 2:46 NIV). After the year 70, it became clear to them that they would never again "continue to meet together in the temple". They would never again hear the psalms of David being sung in Hebrew in the right way. They would soon disobey the ritual rules of clean and unclean and start eating pork as the most natural thing in the world. The lampstand had indeed been removed. And the first great Christian exodus started, instigated by Paul, who became the creator of Christianity as we know it today, in dialogue with the Greek-Hellenistic culture and the Roman law and religion.

Today Christianity is facing a situation very similar to the situation the first Christians were confronted with in the year 70, when they had to find their way out of a situation, which had deprived them of their natural spiritual basis. As Islam moves west Christianity is moving towards the South. If we are looking for growth, activity and commitment within Christianity, we certainly have to look south.

Transformation of Christianity
Following Lamin Sanneh[5] it could be argued that at its core, Christianity is not a religion; it is a 'translation movement'. When Christianity reaches new people groups, the Bible has to be translated. People have not received the Gospel before they have a copy of the Bible in their native language. With every translation of the Bible, God is given a new name, i.e., the name of God in the given culture. This process of translation is therefore a stage in the serial story of God. By the very fact that God is given many new names, there is a transformation of Christianity. It enters into a new context and it cannot help being affected by this context, which results in a change. Therefore it should not come as a surprise to us to learn that the current movement of Christianity is also a transformation, which is indeed the case. Originally, Christianity as we know it found its shape in a dialogue with Greek and Roman culture and religion. Christianity is now facing a dialogue with philosophical and religious tendencies in the South, which may result in just as radical changes. From this

---

5   Lamin Sanneh, *Translating the Message. The Missionary Impact on Culture.* (Maryknoll: Orbis 1992)

encounter, shapes of Christianity will develop, which we sometimes find difficult to recognize as Christian in a traditional interpretation. But this is a natural development of all religions.

And not just transformation of Christianity; this applies to all religions in the world that they are being transformed by the economic and cultural movement which we designate as 'globalisation'. Religions have become fluid and are on the move. Christianity moves south. Islam goes west and the eastern religions spread all over the place. And when the religions travel they change. This religious change does not happen by way of a dictate from ruling powers. It happens on the individual and personal level. Because it has been prepared with the modern emphasis on the individual, it happens by means of changes in the individual's religious conviction. It does not mean the extermination of Christianity. On the contrary, it grows and changes. But the form of Christianity practiced in the North is facing great problems.

But maybe Europe is an exceptional case? This is in fact what the aforementioned British sociologist of religion Grace Davie argues. In her book she advocates the thesis that Europe is indeed something special. This means that the development that Europe has gone through will probably not repeat itself anywhere else in the world, which we have usually with pride presumed. What we are talking about here is the secularisation thesis.

The relation between modernization and secularisation
The secularisation thesis presumes that economic and social modern-ization leads to secularisation, which in this connection is defined as the withdrawal of religion from the public space. Not necessarily from the private space; secularisation may, on the contrary, lead to privatisation of religion and greater influence on the personal level.

We usually draw a line from the Reformation, over the Enlightenment, to modern times. The Reformation starts the development by questioning the authority of the Catholic Church. This is done by emphasizing the individual, the "pro me" of creation and salvation. What is the meaning of the Creation? It means that God created *me* and all other creatures. This leads to an individualism, which again questions our common basis for religious faith. In addition rationality takes its toll on the religious traditions.

This is the beginning of the end of the sacred canopy, which had so far circumvented the societies. Individualism and reason are emphasized further by means of the Enlightenment. This leads to increased pluralism and secularisation. Secularisation in itself does not lead to a general loss of religion in a globally rationalized society, but to a more general reorganization of the forms of religiosity, itself part of a more general redistribution of beliefs, in a society made structurally uncertain, because of the primacy it gives to innovation and change.[6]

Secularisation was the most important issue of debate among previous generations of western theologians. The impression was widespread that religion was a thing of the past. But the epoch was wrong, as we can see today. There are basic phenomena, which will always require a religious interpretation. Because many believed – with the epoch - that religion was a thing of the past, the awakening to the actual experiences of the power of religion to change the world became especially rude.

From the point of view of systematic theology, secularisation was an exciting concept, which facilitated new and exciting attempts to understand and preach the Christian Gospel. But as far as the Church was concerned, secularisation led to de-Christianisation, which in the long run made it difficult for the Church to survive as more than a service institution. The Protestant ideal of the relation between the Gospel and society is "like sugar in water". The Gospel is the herb that, when dissolved, gives flavour to the drink. On the whole, it has worked like that. Something, however, has not been taken into consideration, namely that - if one wants the flavour to remain in the drink, one must keep and store a reservoir of herbs, a supply of undiluted flavour, which can provide the 'herbs' needed when the course of society has to be adjusted. This was omitted, and therefore secularisation resulted in de-Christianisation.

Statistics show this development in a slackening of the institutional discipline. People are not actively involved with the institution, but they do not abandon their affiliation. People have not stopped believing, but they have stopped letting faith form their lives. Faith

---

6   Daniéle Hervieu-Léger: Secularization, Tradition and New Forms of Religiosity; Some Theoretical Proposals. In Eileen Barker & Margit Warburg (eds.): *New Religions and New Religiosity*. (Aarhus University Press: Aarhus 1998) p.31

becomes a private matter; something personal, which does not exist in the public space.

As Christianity was the prevalent religion, this also meant a de-religionisation or, at least, a dilution of religion to such an extent that it was not always sufficient to satisfy the religious feeling, which was the reason why people looked around for having the empty space filled up. Secularisation and the appearance of the new religious movements thus became interrelated.

How do these new conditions affect the role of religion?

First of all, like everything else in a consumer society, religion becomes a choice. The peculiar thing about pluralism is that it leads to relativisation. When more than one faith is recognized, all religions are being relativised, which again leads to secularisation and indifference. Pluralism brings an increased supply, gives people a choice and thus stimulates "sale". Religion is no longer a matter of necessity, but about choice and preference and seen in connection with choice of life style. Sometimes people make the choice in the dark or they may even take over something by tradition. At other times people will – like in other consumer cases – make an informed choice, by which the function of the religion in the modern society plays an important role. Scholars of sociology have brought forward the terms that religion may take care of the "collective memory", the "common discourse" or the "social capital".

Religion as a collective memory, common discourse or social capital

The French anthropologist Hervieue-Léger sees religion as a form of collective memory. When societies become less based on religion, then, according to Hervieue-Leger's, they are not able to keep the collective memory. She refers to such societies as "amnesic societies", societies with amnesia.[7] Europe lives in a post-Christian culture with amnesia.

Hervieu-Léger sees two trends emerging from this description:
- The growing importance of small groups in the shaping of

7   "Modern societies seem to be more and more unfamiliar with religion; but it is not, as classical secularization theory claims, because they are more and more rational; it is because they are more and more amnesic, because they are less and less able to develop a living collective memory as a source of meaning for the present and orientations for the future." D. Hervieu-Léger, 1998, p.38

religious identities. Such small groups provide the individual believers with communal confirmation of their own meaning system. Believing is deciding or inventing that we are engendered. And secondly:
- The spreading of relativism, which follows from the symbiosis between religious pluralism and the modern culture of the individual, tends to create or recreate a new call for denominational identification.

Others mention that we have lost our common discourse. What might replace such a common discourse? We can observe what are on people's minds. That is money, sex, pop culture and sports. Consumerism is in many ways the new religion, but most people can only satisfy their hunger once, so they start looking around for things to fill in the empty space. Especially, sports and entertainment are becoming to many a replacement for religion. Sport arenas around the world are today the scenes of great solidarity and roar of atmosphere, and we see innovations in the rituals that have to do with sports.

This still leaves the unsolved question: What provides the coherence of societies? Can consumerism and entertainment fulfil that role? "Panem et circenses" (bread and entertainment) was also the order of the day in the late Roman Empire; and we know how they fared. Religion has in many societies played the role of giving coherence and identity to a given society. The Church used to and can in certain cases still administer part of this social capital in today's society, but the share is declining and declining fast because faith does not lead to commitment and taking responsibility. People are believing without belonging. This development co-exists in the Nordic countries with a parallel growing tendency of belonging without believing. People stay in the church, pay their church tax but do not really care. Lutheranism has become in countries such as Denmark a sort of civil religion.

And the future?
I have rehearsed how I interpret the situation now in order to have a basis for qualified assumptions of how the development will proceed. The future depends on the choices we make now. And the most obvious choice we are confronted with now is a choice between a future characterized by a "clash of civilisations" or a peaceful multiethnic, multicultural and multi-religious coexistence.

In Western Europe the mainline churches are in decline, sometimes in a dramatic decline. Both St. Peter's in Rome and St. Paul's Cathedral in London have the same ground plan as Hagia Sofia. We are far from a situation where St. Peter and St Paul is confronted with the same fate as their sister church in Constantinople/Istanbul. It was turned into a mosque three days after the Ottoman siege in 1453. But in a hundred to two hundred years time span? Taking into account the dramatic changes that has taken place within the latest 40 years one could not be altogether sure.

But the fate of Christianity in Western Europe is however only one paradigm among many for the future of Christianity. Europe represents – so it seems – a special case (Grace Davie). Although Christianity is declining in the West, we see major growth in Asia (Korea, China), resurgence in Africa, and transformation in Latin America. The pattern is similar: forms of Christianity originally planted in the region by Europeans or North Americans were taken over by an indigenous leadership and went on to flourish in new forms. Therefore – and that is our *first* conclusion concerning the future of global Christianity - it is unlikely that there will be one normative Christianity at the global level; rather Christianity will experience very different futures in its various global manifestations.[8]

Why is Christianity growing in the South?
Paradoxically it seems to be happening in the wake of decolonisation. The end of colonial period seems to have spurred the growth of Christianity.

But what is it that draws people to Christ in the Two Thirds World? To get a true answer to that we need to listen to people who come out of this environment. One is Lamin Sanneh that sums up his description of Africa in the following: "Removal of colonialism as a stumbling block, delayed effect of Bible translation into indigenous language, African leadership and initiative and the preservation of the

---

8   "Christianity, while surviving the twenty-first century, will undergo major changes, most
    significantly as a result of the continued expansion of Christianity in the non-western
    world and its likely diminishing role in the west… Its future lies in the largely
    unreported growth in Africa and Asia. In the west we may hear little more than the
    melancholy low roar of an ebbing tide. Yet elsewhere the tide is flowing and new
    possibilities emerging." Alister E. McGrath: *The Future of Christianity*. (Blackwell
    Publisher: Oxford 2002) p.118f.

indigenous names of God."[9]

From an Asian perspective the Singaporean theologian Hwa Yung points to three factors: 1. Signs and wonders within Pentecostal-charismatic Christianity. 2. The gospel's power to change individual and personal circumstances. 3. Socio-political transformation and nation building in the modern world.[10]

Characteristic of those trends are that they are, if not opposed to, then at least very different from, a western naturalistic and mechanistic view of the world rooted in enlightenment values such as empiricism and rationalism. Within that worldview all supernatural tendencies are rejected. But Christians from the non-western world read the Bible through their own worldview lens and find great similarities between their worldview and that of the bible and they are open to "signs and wonders". Thus manipulations of the miraculous in healing and other forms of deliverance have an impact on the spread of Christianity. Another reason why many in the non-western world are turning to Christianity is its perceived power to change the individual and personal circumstances. Many conversion stories are recounted around a scheme of genuine transformation. And the gospel is not seen only as something that can change individual circumstances. Liberation and socio-political change has for a long time been at the centre of gospel proclamation and increasingly the gospel is seen as providing a spiritual foundation for the moral and cultural rejuvenation needed for building a new society.

Many leaders and intellectuals in the two thirds world are wrestling with the challenge of social and economic modernisation. In their search for an adequate foundation for a society characterized by justice, equality, freedom, economic prosperity and political stability, they encounter the spiritual and religious roots of these phenomena. And many come to see the relationship between concepts of freedom of conscience, human rights, the rule of law and other foundational concepts in western liberal democracy to their roots in Christianity that undergirds them.

---

9   Lamin Sanneh: *Whose Religion is Christianity? The Gospel beyond the West*. (William B. Eerdmans. Grand Rapids 2003), p.19.
10 *The integrity of mission in the light of the gospel*. Paper given at NIME research course, Denmark, March 2005

When the foundational concepts of liberal democracy fail to emerge in many non-western societies it is because there is no adequate basis of reason for it to do so. The role of Christianity for the emergence of liberal democracy has not been sufficiently recognized. Hwa Yung concludes: "The evidence from the ground level demonstrates that hundreds of millions have found meaning, hope, healing from disease, deliverance from bondage to and fear of the powers of darkness, upward social mobility, adequate foundations for nation-building and new communities, and ultimately forgiveness of sin and eternal life … They have found Christ to be the answer to their deepest needs and longings." (p.12).

Other implications will be that Christianity in the two-thirds-world will be challenged to find and formulate their own self-identity. That will happen through a critique of the western worldview that will be accused of being dualistic, separating soul and body, spirit and matter. Western Christianity will have to come to terms with their guilt complex and it will be forced to re-evaluate its enlightenment shaped worldviews and consequently their own theological formulations. Much will depend on whether it will be possible to develop an adequate theology of religious plurality. The reigning pluralism which is a cover for extreme relativism will not do, because it first of all will not satisfy the growing Churches in the South.

From Luther to McDonald
What trends will then be formative in the next church?
John Henry Newman is reported to have said: If the church is to remain the same, it must change. So we should expect changes. It will naturally be a different church that will survive. For instance will the traditional denominations be of less importance? As a community of a nondenominational character the next church will eschew the Byzantine labyrinth of ecclesiastical standpoints and politics. The influence of globalisation will contribute to the marketing of Christianity and the McDonaldization of the church.[11] From this follow two trends:
- One will lead to *diversity* and variety. Contemporary sociology describes how modern societies are fragmented in state, market, civic society and individualized life forms. The church will

---

11   John Drane: *The McDonaldization of the Church: Spirituality ,Creativity and the Future of the Church.* (DTL: London 2000)

feel compelled to respond to the different segments of society, and thus in responding to these different segments it takes on different shapes.

- Another trend will lead to a certain kind of *uniformity*. What is characteristic of McDonald is its efficiency, calculability, predictability and control. So we will see churches that very efficiently try to market their message in a calculable, predictable and controlled ways.

From consensus ecumenism to theology of religions

Plurality we have; unity we seek. This old adage in the ecumenical movement is strengthened in the future. Ecumenical theology will get a new urgency. Not the old consensus *oikoumene*. Select theologians coming together and producing texts that are of relevance for nobody, that activity will diminish. As denominational differences diminish there will be an urgent need to widen the ecumenical perspective and include the religions. Of course there will be churches refusing to have anything to do with each other and other religious communities. By this approach a specific group can have the benefit of maintaining a doctrinal integrity and thus protect a Christian orthodoxy, but in the long run it will be detrimental also to the group's survival. Therefore the only option left is to acknowledge the differences and in spite of what is open to collaboration, maybe only on a limited number of issues. The importance of doctrinal differences is bound to diminish in view of the attacks on Christian belief from secularism, consumerism, materialism and other religions.

The religious encounter happens everywhere, and the churches need to be ready to discuss all the inherited doctrinal formulations. Plurality we have, - also here. Some will from the descriptive plurality draw the pluralistic consequence that everything is relative. Others will opt for a syncretistic form of Christianity arguing – with a certain right – that Christianity has always been syncretistic. Others again will favour fundamentalist versions. That is one of the most disturbing points in the present situation that fundamentalism is growing within all the major world religions. And here we who are students of religion and religious studies scholars have a problem, because we normally do not like fundamentalism. John Hick labels fundamentalism an "inferior religion". But what we do not like, it is hard for us to understand.

Conflict and peace.

That brings us to the question of war and peace. It goes without saying that the mentioned development here could lead to increased conflict. In Europe the Westphalia principle "cujus regio ejus religio" for a period of several hundred years served as a peacekeeping tool. Freedom of religion, the mother of all human rights, brings again disturbance and unrest to the area. Freedom of religion is still a utopian dream in many parts of the world. Freedom of religion is to me a part of our heritage from the enlightenment that we cannot give up and need to enforce vigorously. That means that there is a potential conflict here when the demand for religious freedom is hampered by regimes or religions that are not open to and welcoming conversions. Freedom of religion is not just the freedom to have your religion, but also the ability to shift and change religion without civic consequences. No hindrance for the free exercise of religion and religious change can be accepted unless a certain religion causes harm to the individual. A growing form of violence is religious persecution.[12]

In addition there has been an escalation of violence in today's world. Since the early 1990s wars in and among failed nation-states have killed close to eight million people and made refugees of an additional four million. Hundreds of millions have been left impoverished, malnourished, and deprived of fundamental needs for security, health care, and education. We have witnessed genocide of whole ethnic groups (Rwanda and Sudan). And failed nation states have been breeding ground for instability and mass-migration and reservoirs and exporters of terror.

The religions are called to respond to such escalations. Humanitarian aid to the victims is one ongoing response. The World Council of Churches have instituted a Decade to Overcome Violence (2001-2010), an effort through the use of non-violent tactics to overcome the violence of division in our societies and to respond to the yearning for peace and a life of dignity for future generations.

Several states have seen the necessity to work with reconciliation in order to move forward towards a more peaceful state. Most prominently the South African Truth and Reconciliation Commission.

---

12 Barrett and Johnson estimated that there would be 169.000 Christian martyrs in 2005 with an increase to 210.000 per year by 2025. Status of Global Mission 2005. IBMR 29/1, 2005, p.29.

Originally a secular response to the scars of apartheid, the commission became a Christian effort against injustice under the leadership of Archbishop Desmond Tutu.

Here at the end I will point to some elements in the Christian tradition that can contribute to a peaceful development.

- The Jesus figure and the stories that document his non-violent and peaceful approach to the neighbour.
- The strong tradition for pacifism within Christianity
- The ability to distinguish between the inner and outer sphere, the spiritual and the secular, religion and politics.
- The foundation for a firm ethical grounding builds on the notion of reconciliation.

Reconciliation will be the most important task for the religions amid the violence of this century. Here the Christian tradition has something to offer. Let me end by referring to Robert Schreiter's understandings of the Christian message of reconciliation.

- First it is God who initiates and brings about reconciliation. Both victims and oppressors are invited to co-operate in God's reconciling ways.
- Second, reconciliation is more a spirituality than a strategy. It needs to become a vocation or way of life and not a set of discrete tasks to be performed.
- Third, reconciliation makes of both victim and oppressor a new creation. It is not just righting wrongs or restoring a past state.
- Fourth, it is the passion, death and resurrection of Jesus that in the end overcomes the experience of conflict and violence
- Finally, reconciliation embraces all dimensions of reality. It both breaks down human enmity and embraces the entire cosmos.[13]

---

13 Robert J. Schreiter: *Reconciliation: Mission and Ministry in a changing Social order.* (Orbis. Maryknoll, N.Y. 1992). See also Norman E. Thomas: Radical Mission in a Post 9/11 World: Creative Dissonances. IBMR 29/1, p.2ff.

THEOLOGICAL EDUCATION FOR THE NEXT CHRISTENDOM

Stephen Spencer

In the concluding chapter of *The Next Christendom* Philip Jenkins writes powerfully of the need for Christians in this new century to gain a better understanding not only of Islam but of one another:

> ...perhaps the more pressing need is to appreciate that other religious giant, the strangely unfamiliar world of the new Christianity. Southern Christianity, the Third Church, is not just a transplanted version of the familiar religion of the older Christian states: the New Christendom is no mirror image of the Old. It is a truly new and developing entity. Just how different from its predecessor remains to be seen (p.214).

This statement and Jenkins' book as a whole is significant because it is describing the emergence of a new historic paradigm of Christianity that does not sit happily with the modern liberal paradigm of the northern churches. The potential for misunderstanding and painful conflict in this new century is huge (as the Anglican Communion already knows) and the need for achieving some measure of mutual understanding is increasingly urgent.

What does all this imply for the churches of the north as they seek to serve God's mission in partnership with the churches of the south? How are they to respond to the increasingly inescapable pluralism of the contemporary religious scene? Secondly, how are they to respond in the way they educate, train and form their ministers and priests? The first question is one that every Christian needs to face. The second question is one that I am keen to address as a tutor on an ordination course that prepares men and women for ministry in the Church of England and Methodist Church.

Local ministry

Starting with the first question it is important to recall the way recent missiological literature has focussed attention on two key concepts, evangelism and dialogue. It is generally argued that the church should both proclaim the reign of Christ in word and deed, whether at a personal or a corporate level, *and* be committed to open-ended listening and learning from those of different faiths. But there is clearly a significant tension between these two concepts. David Bosch's *Transforming Mission* highlights the tension in recent official documents:

> "We observe it in the Vatican II documents, for instance. Two affirmations, which seem to be mutually incompatible, speak to us from these documents – God's universal salvific will and the possibility of salvation outside the church *versus* the necessity of the church and of missionary activity. The same unresolved tension emerges from *Mission and Evangelism* [the WCC document of 1982], which states, on the one hand, that the proclamation of God's reign in Christ is at the very heart of the church's vocation in the world and, on the other hand, that "the Spirit of God is constantly at work in ways that pass human understanding and in places that to us are least expected"... (pp.488-9).

Bosch then offers some reflections on this tension, and his words begin to sketch how the church today can respond to its pluralist context:

> "Such language boils down to an admission that we do not have all the answers and are prepared to live within the framework of penultimate knowledge, that we regard our involvement in dialogue and mission as an adventure, are prepared to take risks, and are anticipating surprises as the Spirit guides us into fuller understanding. This is not opting for agnosticism, but for humility. It is, however, a bold humility – or a humble boldness. We know only in part, but we do know. And we believe that the faith we profess is both true and just, and should be proclaimed" (p.498).

The local church, then, is to see its theological understanding of the Christian faith as inhabiting a *penultimate* place. This means it is not to see its convictions as simply expendable in its encounter with other faiths or with Jenkins' Third Church. When North American liberal-minded Anglicans talk to bishops from Nigeria, for example, they are not simply to relinquish their convictions about sexuality in response to the demands of a Third World church. But nor are they to regard their convictions as non-negotiable certainties, the ultimate knowledge of the kingdom. One side is not to surmount and negate what the other brings to the dialogue, but nor is it to cave into pressure without a dialogue of equal partners taking place. As Bosch memorably puts it, dialogue and proclamation are an adventure in which both sides must be prepared to take risks and expect to be surprised by what the Spirit reveals.

This is not an easy place to be: *how* do you proclaim your faith boldly while genuinely listening to the other? Vincent Donovan in *Christianity Rediscovered* provides a well known and vivid example. At the start of his time as a missionary in Tanzania he famously decided to leave his mission station with its church, classrooms and clinic, and approach the Masai people on foot, with just an interpreter, quite vulnerable, engaging them in dialogue in their own language, with the posing of questions and the offering of his own answers, giving them the space to accept or reject what he was saying. There was something significant about his manner of approach, showing that he was bringing his theology not with power but as a gift that could be accepted or rejected. Furthermore the dialogue itself formed and influenced what he was saying. One memorable passage describes how he and the new Masai Christians searched for the right term in the Masai language to describe the role of the priest. The term offered by the Masai villagers themselves, *ilaretok*, meaning a helper who brings a community together, was an unexpected choice and changed the meaning of the role itself, removing the ideas of preacher, pray-er, prophet and sacramentalist. The Masai wanted these roles to be taken up by the community as a whole in a corporate way (pp.157-8). The community-building role was regarded as the key contribution of the priest. So the dialogue and proclamation were clearly influencing each other, and in a creative way.

Donovan writes in the preface that his book is as much about inter-acting with American youth as with the Masai and so has a wider significance. It shows a simple yet powerful model of engaging in dialogue and proclamation at the same time. It provides an example of the kind of ministry advocated by Rowan Williams in an address to the General Synod of the Church of England in July 2004 at the height of divisions over sexuality. He called for a kind of leadership which is 'very clear about theological priorities, not protective of its status, skilled in listening and in interpreting what may seem very different language groups to each other.'(p.5).

Types of theological education

This leads on to the second question, which is about how a church can educate, train and form men and women to lead its people in this venturesome mixture of dialogue and mission.

The traditional model of theological education looked to a seminary to provide everything that was needed. The student was removed from their home environment and placed in a residential college for a number of years. They were therefore removed from those markers that gave them a sense of place, belonging, skill and experience. They were placed in a setting where their identity was formed by the seminary itself, sometimes by having to wear the same type of clothing, and where they were treated as a kind of empty receptacle. The education and training was predominantly through the declamation of lectures, in order to fill this receptacle with the different elements of the curriculum, like pouring water into a jug. This would allow the newly ordained minister to 'pour out' the contents of that curriculum during their subsequent ministry. It could be described as the *monist* approach to training – the content of the training was provided entirely by the seminary, as a kind of monologue.

While this approach had some undoubted merits, including the provision of a solid grounding in the literature, history and doctrine of the respective tradition of that seminary, it did not equip students for encountering and learning from other traditions and other faiths. They were provided with a system of belief and practice that was all encompassing: the possibility that other traditions might have something to teach them was not recognised.

Contemporary theological education has generally moved away from this approach. There is now a much greater recognition of the importance of an interactive process in the learning that takes place. A text such as Laurie Green's *Let's Do Theology* is a well known example, where the theological student begins their learning by recalling their own experience, possibly in some crisis or challenging situation, and then goes to their ecclesial tradition in its scriptures, history and doctrine, to explore the resources it offers for facing that crisis or challenge. The teachers on the course provide the necessary guidance on what to read and how to engage in research in the tradition, responding to the questions and interests of the student. Then, at the next stage of the process, the student reflects on what they have found, sifting and appraising the material they have uncovered and discerning how it shapes an appropriate way of responding to the crisis or challenge. This can be a life-changing experience as the student discovers new and radical perspectives on their situation. Finally they move from reflection to action, where they seek to put into practice what they have learnt. During this phase new challenges and crises may occur, prompting the whole process to begin once again.

Green calls this methodology the pastoral cycle. It is an approach that draws on the action-reflection model of Paulo Freire and Liberation Theology and the educational theory of Kolb's learning cycle.

Many ministerial courses in the UK identify their mode of learning with this kind of approach. It has many merits, one of which is to deliberately draw upon the learning and experience that students bring with them to the course. The background life of mature students often provides rich material for reflective theology. Indeed with mature students this is especially important as they are generally not willing to be treated as empty receptacles! And the outcome of the learning process is practical as well as theoretical: the student goes back to the crisis or challenge that they faced with a fresh way of responding.

But there is an important limitation to this approach. Is not the exploration of their own ecclesial tradition too narrow an aim in a context where the need for dialogue and understanding across traditions and faiths is paramount? Is it not too individualistic for the dialogue to be only between the student's own experience and the respective ecclesial tradition? Does the dialogue not need to include a third party, 'the other', a representative of a strange and different point of view?

Many theological courses already include an element of encounter with other faiths in their curriculum, often in a module on interfaith relationships or urban mission. But this is not sufficient to meet the challenges Jenkins and Bosch are describing, because it compartmentalises the encounter. The encounter with 'the other' needs to affect not just certain aspects of the curriculum but the whole approach and structure of the curriculum itself. The new Christendom, or Third Church, as described by Jenkins, is challenging fundamentally the whole paradigm of belief and practice of the Northern churches, as does Islam and other world faiths in different kinds of way. The type of dialogue that Bosch is advocating will affect much more than one or two discrete modules.

The mode of delivery in theological education therefore needs to be not just a bi-polar dialogue but a tri-polar dialogue or, in other words, a *trialogue*, with the student representing one of the parties, the course and its background ecclesial tradition another, and 'the other' a third.

This 'other' needs to be a person or a group who is significantly different and strange, who does not think within the same paradigm and is going to challenge the presuppositions and the language of the other two parties at every point.

Vincent Donovan might again provide an illustration of what this means. He describes the way that when he went into the Masai villages he was not just taking a gospel message but was entering into a process of discovery about the nature of the gospel in this setting. In important ways his own theological education was taking place and it is important to note there were three influences at work: firstly, the Roman Catholic tradition that he had been trained within and that he represented when he came into the Masai villages - Donovan is clear that he stood within this tradition and wanted to pass it on; secondly, his own opinions and outlook which were especially influenced by the writings of Roland Allen; and, thirdly, the outlook of the Masai villagers themselves, shaped by their own animist beliefs and daily struggle to live, which influenced his thinking in radical and powerful ways and took him beyond traditional missionary work. He was willing to let the 'otherness' of the Masai have a crucial role in his own theological education, to the extent that he eventually formulated an African Creed which is printed at the back of his book. Donovan's example, whatever we might think of the outcome, is a model of what trialogue may look like.

Learning and teaching
Returning to the topic of theological education we can ask how trialogue might be expressed in a course of ministerial training today. And here an important initial point is that we do not have to abandon the pastoral cycle but, rather, to widen it to include three parties rather than two. As mentioned, dialogue should not be confined to the 'other faiths' part of the syllabus but be an integral part of the whole curriculum, so that trialogue happens at every stage. As the student engages in Biblical studies, historical and doctrinal modules, pastoral theology, ethics, etc, they will not just relate their exploration and reflection to their own situation and experience but allow the outlook of 'the other', whether from another faith or from the new Christendom, to shape and affect how they understand the faith. *Who* the other is may not be crucial: a range of different faiths and outlooks will be encountered during a lifetime of ministry and a theological course cannot prepare a future minister for every

eventuality. It is more important that the discipline of taking 'the other' seriously, whoever they may be, is formed within the student. It is the habitual practice of this discipline that needs to be fostered.

How might this happen? On the Northern Ordination Course we tried one approach at a recent eight day residential Easter School. This paper will conclude with a description of what happened during the week in order to present an example of trialogue in practice.

The theme of the week was 'Christian Mission in a Plural World'. In the planning process the staff quickly decided that the four stages of the learning or pastoral cycle (experience, exploration, reflection, action) would provide a good framework for the week. Students would be encouraged to move through each stage as they engaged with the theme. But what kind of experience would be the best starting point? When the subject of mission is broached the tendency in Anglican circles, at least, has been to start thinking of 'my church and how can it reverse the decline in attendance?' The issue of mission becomes framed within narrow institutional terms related to a parochial context. The importance of trialogue, on the other hand, is that it stops this happening by placing issues in a broader context. For the Easter School the staff decided that an encounter with other faiths, especially Islam and Hinduism in the city of Bradford, would be a key part of the week. And then, knowing that this was the case, it became clear that the starting point for the week would need to be the poor state of relationships between Christianity and these other faiths since the events of 9/11. Questions of mission could not be addressed until this background issue had been investigated. So the very fact of including interfaith encounter within the week influenced its starting point and development.

The week itself included lectures on the history of interfaith relations, explorations of the theology of the other faiths, visits to a temple and mosque hosted by welcoming and articulate members of those places of worship, viewing the film 'Yasmin' (about inter-generational relationships in a Pakistani Muslim family), Bible studies and presentations on contemporary theological Christian responses to other faiths, and discussion and reflection groups. The climax of the week was the activity of each student group producing an exhibition and written commentary to express their response to the question 'what, then, is Christian mission in this plural context?' So the week moved from experience, through exploration and reflection, to action.

The students produced a thoughtful and exciting set of responses to the week. The exhibitions were carefully and beautifully constructed and, along with the commentary, showed a sustained answer to the question. Many of the commentaries included Christological, soteriological, ecclesiological and eschatological themes within their missiological response, and so demonstrated impressive expressions of systematic theology, drawing on Scripture and tradition as well as the encounters of the week. While some responses expressed an exclusivist type of theology, and others an inclusivist type, and others a pluralist type (reflecting the different backgrounds of the students), they were all coherent and vivid in what they were saying. They demonstrated that the students had engaged in the kind of risky and adventurous combination of dialogue and proclamation that we saw Bosch advocate.

A number of the students later commented that the week had been the most powerful and transformative educational experience they had had on the course. All the feedback, remarkably, was positive.

At the end I was left wondering why the whole of the three year course could not be like this: why could the eight day process not be expanded to cover three years? Why could the encounter with 'the other' not be a systemic part of the whole course? Why could not trialogue, within the context of the pastoral cycle, be the basic epistemology of ministerial training? The burden of this paper has been to argue that it should be so.

References

Bosch, David, *Transforming Mission: Paradigm Shifts in Theology of Mission,* Orbis 1991
Donovan, Vincent J., *Christianity Rediscovered: An Epistle from the Masai,* SCM 1982
Jenkins, Philip, *The Next Christendom: The Coming of Global Christianity,* Oxford 2002
Williams, Rowan, 'Presidential Address to the General Synod of the Church of England', 14th July 2003, available on www.archbishopofcanterbury

Part II

ISSUES FOR EUROPE

WHY CHRISTIAN EXPERIENCE IN EUROPE MATTERS

Werner Ustorf

There is indeed no way to deny the marginalization of the Church in Western Europe.[1] But I find the language of death that has in places been used, often triumphantly, more than a little dubious. The smugness with which Europe's churches are declared dead might even conceal an implicit desire to take over their inheritance. Churches are institutions, at least in a historical and sociological sense, not biological entities. Their life force is in the people, whether they are in or outside the institution. People die; whereas institutions lose their function or usefulness. Therefore, it is not the Church with a capital C that dies, not "God" or "Christianity". It is rather that the churches, as inherited and forms of Christian social organization are increasingly losing their usefulness. But this is very different from pronouncing the end of Christianity. The rhetoric of decline is prone to obscure the processes of social change and religious transformation. It seems as well it works in conjunction with yesterday's image of a powerful religious institution and that while it refers to both the friends and the enemies of the dream of Christendom, it has very little to offer those who have other dreams (such as the dream of an authentic and

---

1   Hugh McLeod, *Secularisation in Western Europe, 1848-1914*, London: Macmillan, 2000; Callum Brown, *The Death of Christian Britain. Understanding Secularisation 1800-2000*, London: Routledge, 2001; Steve Bruce, *God is Dead: Secularization in the West*, Oxford: Blackwell, 2002; Grace Davie, *Religion in Modern Europe: A Memory Mutates*, Oxford: OUP, 2000; Robin Gill, *The 'Empty' Church Revisited*, Ashgate, 2003. H. McLeod and W. Ustorf [eds.], *The Decline of Christendom in Western Europe, 1750-2000*, CUP, 2003.

distinctly European form of Christianity). In his book on the coming of a new Christendom Philip Jenkins makes it abundantly clear that the particularly Western form of Christianity, namely liberal Christianity, is not his dream. Rather, liberal Christianity is said to be *irrelevant* to the great majority of people and is in a state of collapse. It is, therefore, best that it be disregarded here, now, and everywhere.[2]

Unfortunately, Jenkins does not properly define liberal Christianity, and it is therefore anybody's guess as to what has and has not been drawn into the abyss of liberalism. It does seem, however, that he has in particular two things in mind: questions of personal morality, such as those surrounding abortion and homosexuality, and the issue of the over-intellectualization of the Christian tradition, including historical exegesis and the pursuance of any philosophical inquiry into the foundations of the faith. If one took the pain of these struggles away from Christianity what would be left? One would end up not with a living faith, but instead a system of safe knowledge; the world of the past kept artificially apart from the present, and, more irritatingly still, a sort of theological truth that is both ready-made and therefore instantly available and *in extremis* even usable as a weapon. My point is not that liberal Christianity must not be criticized. Critical statements about the irrelevance of much of western theology we need to hear and, indeed, have heard. For example, the *Ecumenical Association of Third World Theologians*, in the 1970s, was most outspoken about western theology's failure to address the scandals of imperialism and global inequality.[3] But Jenkins' critique is different. He does not advocate liberation theology or a radical change in what might be described in a global context as the theological terms of trade; instead, he urges a move towards orthodox conservatism. Whether this will make Christianity in the West more relevant can be doubted.

But it is perhaps more fruitful in this respect to ask 'of which particular group does the issue of relevance actually apply?'[4] Jenkins

---

2   Philip Jenkins, *The Next Christendom. The Coming of Global Christianity*, Oxford, New York: OUP, 2002, passim, in particular 196-198, 214-218.
3   Cp. for EATWOT the *SCM Dictionary of Third World Theologies*, ed. by V. Fabella and R.S. Sugirtharajah, London: SCM, 2003.
4   Relevance is one of those concepts that presupposes a specific context and, at the same time, other contexts that are distinctively different. If relevance is defined primarily in relation to a specific context, its value or non-value cannot simply be decided by criteria derived from other contexts. Rather, it is likely that one specific variant of Christian experience has no immediate relevance elsewhere. Theologically or systematically,

responds to this question by producing a chapter of statistics in which the growth of non-liberal Christianity is shown to be outstripping that of the liberal tradition. Relevance is therefore defined – though from the not-so-secure vantage point of the year 2050 - by simple numbers and a process of teleological verification. In such circumstances, with the liberal-Christian dinosaur now seen to be lumbering towards almost certain extinction, should we not ourselves simply go with the ideological flow and accept that the tradition is really little more than one of history's many failed evolutionary offshoots?

My position is that we cannot and indeed must not attempt to escape from the questions that our culture is asking. It is far better to admit that Christianity in its traditional or liberal form does not have answers to some of the questions than to offer orthodox answers to questions that nobody is asking. Historically, it is clear that an orthodox answer is always the repetition of yesterday's cultural-theological consensus or compromise. But this consensus may no longer convince when the cultural and historical context has changed. What is needed is a new interpretation. Since 1943, that is, since the publication of Yvan Daniel and Henri Godin's *La France, Pays de Mission?* (France, a mission country?)[5] and, subsequently, with the emergence of the Worker-Priest Movement, we have known that no missionary approach towards the post-Christian cultures of Europe could possibly start from within existing church structures. It has, rather, to be a radical and independent approach - free, like those Jesuit missionaries who worked in Spanish and Portuguese colonies, but who did so independently of the colonial clergy that had been subject to the *padroado*, meaning that they were appointed by and answerable to the crown. Or, in Daniel and Godin's words, the mission to the metal workers of Renault was to follow the model of Paul's mission to the dockers of Corinth, or that of the missionary instruction given by Pope Gregory the Great[6] to Augustine when he embarked on his mission to Britain around 600.[7] The methods and the aim of this mission have to

---

however, every variant of Christian history and every individual case of relevance represents a question to all the others.

5   Edition used here: Lyon: Les Editions de l'Abeille, 1943.
6   The text is readily available. Three examples: J.N. Hillgarth, *Christianity and Paganism 350-750*, Philadelphia: UPP, 1989, 152f.; Richard Fletcher, *The Conversion of Europe from Paganism to Christianity 371-1386 AD*, London: HarperCollins, 1997; also Book I, Chapter 30 of Bede's *Ecclesiastical History of the English People*, Penguin, London 1990, 91-93.
7   Daniel/Godin, 93, 112, 115, 125.

be rigorously indigenous and charitable - however, as Daniel and Godin insist, it is a hands-on-type of charity, one that would be realized in and through struggle.[8] Mission in the West cannot mean the reintegration of runaway cultures within pre-existing ecclesiological and theological boundaries. And driving people back into church could actually be a mistake - this was indeed the problem with most of the reconversion projects that have been launched since the 1950s. Any new conception of mission compels the discovery of a completely new understanding of what it is to be Christian while engaging with the dominant powers. Missionary rhetoric that is based on the magic of revival or a return to orthodoxy is not indigenous and charitable, because its primary function is self-concerned, namely, either to satisfy a Christian sub-culture's need to establish a distinct public identity, or to use faith not only for the defence of, but also, when required, for the return to, a particular form of political order.[9]

The argument I am putting forward here is actually not unlike the one that Jenkins has used in order to illustrate the authenticity of the faith elsewhere, namely in the *South*. Faith becomes authentic, he says, when it relates to a specific context and expresses itself in its own cultural language. Liberal Christianity, I think, despite all its shortcomings and the disasters it helped to create in the twentieth century in particular, was one such authentic expression of the faith in a context of fundamental cultural and political change. Theologically – from Friedrich Schleiermacher to Paul Tillich - it has opened up a wide space in which it was, and still is, possible to explore matters of faith as modern Europeans. What does this mean? Among other things, it creates a context in which faith is engaged in a permanent conversation with reason and more particularly with the forces of secularization. These forces produced their own theory: for a century the "master narrative" of the secularization theory was dominant in sociology, history, and the political and religious sciences. This theory, which was indeed believed by progressive theologians and missiologists and, then, applied globally, says roughly the following: due to modernization there is a long-term and inevitable historical decline in the social significance of religion, a trend which, though it may be accelerated by certain short-term processes such as

8   A "charité 'à faire', à réaliser dans la lutte". Ibid. 207.
9   Cp. John Kent's analysis of Victorian revival movements, *Holding the Fort*, London 1978.

72

industrialization, could also be interrupted by others, such as periodic religious revivals. Many of our research perspectives, as well as our conceptual toolboxes, have been shaped by this theory. In a time which heralds the "return of religion", both at home and abroad, this is a problem, and the secularization hypothesis needs to be modified or deconstructed altogether. There are, it must be said, other models around at this moment, such as the thesis which portrays religion as marketplace or economy, and which, if I am not mistaken, Jenkins applies to his prognosis of world Christianity. Therefore, although the theory, that is, the great western narrative of secularization, may be wrong, it has to be conceded that the processes of secularization do indeed happen. There seems to be a real net loss now of established religious tradition in Europe.

Liberal Christianity is inculturated in this secular historical context. However, like many institutions of secular culture, for example, the universities, liberal Christianity and its churches have been caught unguarded by the return of religion. The liberal response to the gospel is still very much present in the academy, even more so in the fields of charity and social care, but it is no longer universally accepted, not even in Europe. It seems its parameters are simply too narrow to contain the new quest for spiritual discovery. Yet it allows many if not most of the inhabitants of European culture to read the gospel narratives on the basis of powerful cultural paradigms that include such issues as freedom and equality and also to enter into discussion with the ever-growing body of knowledge that is constituted by the humanities and the sciences.

If the hermeneutics of suspicion, which is to say, is the organized application of doubt, really is at the heart of Western culture, if the European understanding of the love of God is expressed socially, and if its dream of freedom is formative in establishing control mechanisms against those in power, including the separation of the religious from the political, and if the conscience of the individual must not be suppressed in the name of the many, then we must say that liberal Christianity is indeed a fitting theological adaptation to the context of modernity. It has been around for more than two centuries and has survived major challenges as well as the many attempts at converting it to orthodoxy or neo-orthodoxy. The death of liberal Christianity has often been proclaimed, but the tradition has turned out to be extremely resilient. The reason for this is the very distinctive way it managed to assimilate the biblical message within the cultural context of European modernity.

No other variant of Christianity has produced such a wealth of reflection and scholarship, nor the sheer range of methodological tools with which to explore the faith. The task surely cannot be to abandon all this, rather, it must be to make this knowledge heard in the ecumenical discussion. I am aware that the missionary movement from the West always had a precarious and ambivalent relationship with liberal Christianity. However, if a European form of Christianity is to survive, now would be a good time to accept this ambivalence and not to reject or exorcise what has made us who we are. The escape from oneself may constitute some momentary relief, but it will not be good enough to stand in the future debates about truth in Christianity. Cultural self-hatred is a bad adviser in religious matters.

I believe these cultural terms of European modernity, for better or worse, have been etched quite deeply into the Christian experience and are, therefore, part of our interior grammar, whether we are liberal, evangelical or charismatic Christians. I think it is better to stay with the culture that we have, and to be critically aware of its insufficiencies, rather than to regress blind-folded towards orthodox conservatism, the mummified truth of yesterday. I will therefore deal with Jenkins' proposal to abandon liberal Christianity by remaining faithful to its context, while at the same time addressing its undoubted weaknesses. I will do this here by discussing two issues that relate to the integrity of the Christian memory: the *first* is a question of what European Christianity has or, perhaps at least, should have learned from its expansion; that is, from the mission history of the last two hundred years. The *second* issue raises a further question about what can be learned from the trauma of the recession of Christianity in Europe today.

1. Learning from mission history:[10]

The last two hundred years of history in general have taught us two very basic lessons: there are doubts as to the reliability of religion as a force for good and a power directed towards the healing and saving of humanity. There are also doubts regarding the reliability of reason as

---

10 A previous version of this summary was published by W. Ustorf, Protestantism and Missions, in: *The Blackwell Companion to Protestantism*, ed. by A. McGrath and D. Marks, Oxford: Blackwell, 2004, 392-402.

the panacea to the world's problems. Reason turned out to be as prone to misuse and temptation as religion proved to be. On both counts our experience is a broken experience. The reconfiguration of faith and reason is a task that is still unfinished and cannot be accomplished, in my view, without facing the brokenness that speaks to us through our history.

Mission work has always been decidedly international and sometimes, even, supra-denominational. On the one hand, this relativized the European settings of the Christian message, on the other, it enabled the *indigenous variants* of Christianity that emerged abroad to develop within a broad ecumenical and, at the same time, genuinely vernacular framework.

In their school activities in particular, missions turned out to be strong advocates of modern culture: they followed the creed of the Enlightenment that insisted that *homo novus*, the new man, could be created through education. Education certainly had aspects of the *tabula rasa* syndrome about it, which is to say, it tended to neglect local knowledge and wisdom, but, simultaneously, it also released impulses that contributed to the subversion of both colonialism and theological dominance. Whether this quest for self-governance was a genuine expression of the *power of Christ* or had its origins in the Enlightenment paradigm of *equality* is a different question.[11] It has been said that the great projects of the West, namely the unification of the world through either secular rationality or religion, have both run aground. But this does not relieve us of the task of assessing the intimate connection between the two.

The translation of the bible into the vernacular created the conditions in which Christianity could break free from its western cultural moorings. The result was an incredible diversification of ecclesiological models and theological approaches. This transformed Christian identity and contributed to the end of Christendom or of the European phase in the life of Christianity.[12] Its repercussions on Europe, first in the

---

11 Cp. B. Stanley (ed.), *Christian Missions and the Enlightenment*, Grand Rapids: Eerdmans, 2001; see also W. Ustorf, *Wissenschaft*, Africa and the Cultural Process according to Johann Gottfried Herder (1744-1803), in: *European Traditions in the Study of Religion in Africa*, ed. by F. Ludwig and A. Adogame, Wiesbaden: Harrassowitz, 2004, 117-127.
12 Authors like Andrew Walls, Lamin Sanneh or Philip Jenkins have shown this in much of their work, cp. for example Walls, *The Missionary Movement in Christian History*, Maryknoll: Orbis, 1996, id., *The Cross-Cultural Process in Christian History*, Maryknoll: Orbis, 2001; Sanneh, *Translating the Message. The Missionary Impact on*

academy, are visible, for example, in Walter Hollenweger's programme of intercultural theology. This approach tried to remedy the scandal of restricted access to theological debate. That is, he attacked the privileged theological discourse that the academic tribes of the North Atlantic had established and defended narrative theology, in particular, the oral traditions of the Black churches.[13]

Working with the bible, translating, commenting it, consulting exegetical studies and comparing the text with other sacred texts facilitated a more sophisticated understanding of its contents: sacred texts are not less sacred when we know that they have been written by people with particular interests, biases and dreams. The text itself must not be a fetish. It becomes alive only when the text helps to make the reader understand his or her life in a new way.

The missionary zeal of collecting, describing, analyzing, and classifying non-western knowledge - cultural, ethnological, and religious - did not only deliver the facts that the metropolis needed for control of its remote periphery, it also led to a massive influx of alternative modes of thought into western culture. This influx, however, worked like the "cunning of history" in Hegel's *Philosophy of History*: it ran almost counter to the world mission's efforts to universalize Christianity by undermining still further the collapsed monopoly of Christianity in Europe. The dream of the missions was a religiously homogenized world; the outcome was the multiplication of religious approaches. Mission, by accumulating knowledge about different and often fuller forms of religious expertise, that is expertise not available within Christianity, had become a force of *pluralism*. Not infrequently, the faith of the missionaries was challenged, and some converted. We do know now that – whatever the particular self-image - factually, neither secular rationality nor the Christian faith are universal. They are elements within a much bigger reality.

Culture, Maryknoll: Orbis, 1989; Jenkins, *The Next Christendom. The Coming of Global Christianity*, Oxford: OUP, 2002.

13 Hollenweger's contribution to intercultural theology is less well known than his work in the field of pentecostalism. There is, however, a Festschrift in his honour, edited by Jan Jongeneel, *Pentecost, Mission and Ecumenism. Essays on Intercultural Theology*, Frankfurt/M: P. Lang, 1992. A concise and systematic profile of his intercultural-theological approach has been given by Lynne Price, *Theology out of Place. A Theological Biography of Walter J. Hollenweger*, London: Sheffield Academic Press, 2002.

The problem of pluralism finally began to eat into the missionary assumption that there was, throughout time and space, an unchangeable and known entity called Christianity. This entity, however, could only be a construction, an imagination or a diachronic abstraction. In other words, Christianity was not just horizontally or geographically diverse and unknown, it also replicated this uncertainty historically or vertically. On both counts, the modern Western form of missionary identity appeared to be historically a very specific form of the faith.

The implications of this for one of the central planks of missionary consciousness, namely, the personal relationship with Jesus Christ, were profound. This relationship was effectively a sacralization or a religious transposition of the secular tune of the autonomy of the individual. What became clear now was that no individual experience or form of faith was able to exhaust that of other people, other places and other times. No single life could exhaust the wisdom acquired in other lives, cultures and histories. Unmitigated individualism, whether in faith life or in secular life, came to be seen as a serious problem. Still, the examples of individual Christians, living outside the Church abounded. The thesis that it is impossible to be a Christian outside the community of collective worship is an ecclesial mantra. It is not true. I am one of these outsiders.

Finally, there is a history of missionary hopes, failures and recessions, which embraces not the Promised Land, but rather a reality of loss and exile, and much of this still needs to be written. Recessions, that is, the failures, the dwindling and even the discontinuity of Christianity, are an integral part of the Christian story and as worthy of analysis as any narrative concerning the coming and the growth of Christianity. This is not simply a western question, of course. The Nigerian church historian Ogbu Kalu, for example, wrestles with it as well.[14] He asks, what have the thousands of independent churches and the rich spirituality and religious exuberance that we have witnessed in African Christianity, and that, at the same time, is so much celebrated, envied and instrumentalised in the West, actually done to prevent the continent's swift decline to unprecedented levels of poverty and moral disintegration?

---

14 *Power, Poverty and Prayer*, Frankfurt/M.: P. Lang, 2000.

In brief, the missionary movement from the West is, as the Dutch missiologist Bert Hoedemaker says, not only "the pre-history of ecumenism", a thing of the past perhaps, but much more importantly "the upbeat of a profound learning process in which the Christian tradition was and is truly globalized - in other words: in which Christianity first learned to (re-) interpret its traditions in interaction with other cultures and religions."[15] No theological reflection on today's globalized ethical dilemmas and interreligious relations can afford not to rethink and, perhaps, not to repeat the different steps of this learning process. To be prepared to learn and rethink one's position, and to proceed from Christendom, via the path that takes us from Christianity to Christianness, is a task that is way beyond the choice between orthodox neo-conservatism, liberal "cafeteria religion" and exotic superstition that Jenkins has proposed. The basic question of how to lead a human life in a global world cannot be answered by one tradition alone. What is required is a discussion that is truly intercultural.[16]

2. The experience of marginalization

Currently we are facing a veritable recession of established Christianity in Western Europe. This is partly, as Jenkins knows, due to our demographics and is, so to speak, statistically unavoidable. However, it is also true that the churches have moved to the margins of mainstream culture. A real clash of interests is observable between the church and the people. Christianity and other forms of *big religion* usually want total access to the lives of the people in order to bring about their complete transformation. It appears, however, that this is precisely what many people, probably the majority, do *not* want from their religion. The world religions, but modern rationality as well, try to control and redefine the space that people are continuously carving out for themselves: this is a space where *they*, the people, have the sovereignty of choosing the coping mechanism that best allows them to get through the difficult business of living.

We cannot yet be sure whether this clash means the disintegration of the Christian tradition in Europe or, rather, its transformation into new shapes. But, as said before, the church is not all there is. There is life both inside and outside its confines. It is important to

---

15 In an Email to the author, dated 23/4/2004.
16 Cp. Joseph Ratzinger, *Werte in Zeiten des Umbruchs. Die Herausforderungen der Zukunft bestehen*, Freiburg: Herder, 2005, 36-40.

acknowledge that the battleground where old boundaries (such as secular/religious; church/world) are overstepped and new syntheses and new configurations of the sacred are hammered out, and where the search for the Promised Land continues, is packed with church-leavers. This arena, often the Internet, is the interface of worldviews, of a form of political engagement that seeks the survival of a now fully globalized humanity, and of a multiplicity of religious options. The catchphrase *new spirituality* is just the umbrella term for a whole culture's search for new moorings.[17] An important factor in the religious life of church-leavers seems to be a change in the way they have come to understand and use religion. MacLaren and Heelas/Woodhead believe they have identified a cultural move away from a religiously transcendental mode towards a new type of immanent religion (or spirituality).[18] I am not saying that all is well with this new orientation. All I am saying is that there is a common process that involves the recycling of Christian hope, and that it would indeed be problematic if the churches were to exclude themselves from this.[19] As long as theologians and church hierarchies continue to define Christianity in antithesis to people's religiosity, the gates are firmly closed and we can forget any idea of mission. Wherever Christianity is alive, its shape is precisely a negotiated mix of the Christian tradition and the religious or spiritual space that people have carved out for themselves. It is this negotiation between the teaching of the Church, on the one hand, and people's experiences and narratives, on the other, that also defines the content of words such as God, Jesus or Spirit. I believe that Church and theology can learn from this. The currently observable difficulty of mainline churches in accepting the deep religious and theological transformations in British and European culture in general, and, more specifically, in contemplating their own transformation, is not inevitable.[20] People's stories, experiences and,

---

17 P. Heelas and Linda Woodhead, *The Spiritual Revolution: Why Religion is Giving Way to Spirituality*, Oxford: Blackwell, 2005, are of the opinion that there is a real shift in the way people relate to the divine. They think that the time is over when believers accept their lot as one of submissiveness and obedience to a metaphysical authority - instead they wish to experience the divine as a transformative power within themselves.

18 D. MacLaren, *Mission Impossible: Restoring Credibility to the Church*, Paternoster Press, 2004.

19 Cp. here M. Kroeger, *Im religiösen Umbruch der Welt: Der fällige Ruck in den Köpfen der Kirche*, Stuttgart: Kohlhammer, 2004; Grace Davie, *Religion in Modern Europe: A Memory Mutates*, Oxford: OUP, 2000.

20 Four decades ago, the Dutch missiologist Hans Hoekendijk had already defined this attitude as the churches' "morphological fundamentalism" – a potentially heretical

even, misunderstandings, generate many of the common ideas of a good life, of justice and salvation. Is it so hard to understand that these ideas are also fermenting a new vintage in the Christian wineskin? The common recycling of Christian hope can and ought to take place within the churches themselves. I will give three examples, all taken from recent missiological research.

The *first example* concerns a study of the so-called *youth congregations* in England.[21] This research was conducted entirely within that part of the Church that can be described as evangelical and charismatic and that is now searching for ways of mission that are appropriate for the culture of a post-modern age. What is the specificity of these experimental forms of Christianity that now hope to resonate with popular youth culture? The point is that they all try to include what the American missionary anthropologist Paul Hiebert called "the excluded middle";[22] namely, the world of ancestors, spirits, and invisible powers; the mechanisms for coping with the stages of life, suffering, misfortune and death; and the search for protection, guidance and healing. This world of everyday needs is often excluded from mainline Christianity. These youth congregations reject the institutional church and organize themselves through cell-structures, almost along tribal lines, with a network of teams that allow everyone to participate in leadership. Worship is informal, with a strong emphasis on spiritual experience, and, whether in the form of a rock concert or something more meditative, it is always highly charged. The membership structure is also informal; you belong when you are there. There are no prerequisites, though it is expected that, over time,

---

clinging not to the gospel, but rather to a particular historical expression of Christianity. Recently, the German church historian Matthias Kroeger spoke of the "religiöse Transformationsverweigerung" of the churches – their refusal to open up to the changes going on inside and outside the churches, in particular with respect to the redefinition of "religion", the story of Jesus and basic words such as "God" and "grace". This refusal means also a closing of the gates right in the face of church leavers and alternative believers, giving them no chance to profit from the spiritual treasures Christianity has accumulated over the centuries. Cp. for Hoekendijk now the theological analysis by Frank Petter, *Profanum et Promissio. Het begrip wereld in de missionaire ecclesiologieën van Hans Hoekendijk, Hans Jochen Margull en Ernst Lange*, Groningen theological doctoral thesis, 2002. For Kroeger see his *Im religiösen Umbruch der Welt: Der fällige Ruck in den Köpfen der Kirche*, Stuttgart: Kohlhammer, 2004.

21   Cp. John Hall, *The Rise of the Youth Congregation and its Missiological Significance*, Birmingham PhD thesis, 2003.

22   First published in *Missiology* 10.1 (January 1982); see also now P.G. Hiebert, R.D. Shaw, and T. Tiénou, *Understanding Folk Religion. A Christian response to popular beliefs and practices*, Baker Book House, 1999.

members agree with the core beliefs and values. These core beliefs are surprisingly traditional, and Jenkins would be delighted to hear that. However, the research shows also that the youth congregations failed to make any substantial missionary inroads into the unchurched population. What they did achieve was to keep the children of church attendees in the Church, which itself may have halted or slowed the decline.

The *second example* is taken from research conducted in one of Cardiff's deprived estates. It is based on a very long theological conversation about Life, Church, and God which tool place in a small local congregation.[23] The result is the emergence, "from below", of a true urban theology and one that contains a number of surprising details. It is a theology of exile, in which the Church has been driven away from the centre, where the space outside the Church is theologically fertile, and where God has become strange and unfamiliar. None of the triumphant God-talk of the Christendom era, which still dominates our hymnody, liturgy and ecclesiology, can be used in this situation of exile. Instead, a rethinking is taking place and an exploration into the nature of God has been started. The dominant experience is that God has stepped out of the Church, and that, in order to discern his footsteps, believers and their theology need to follow. It is intriguing to discover that we are dealing here with an experience that is the polar opposite of that which Western missionaries went through: the experience that God was already active before their arrival. This example from Cardiff declaims that God is there, even when the Church has gone.

The *third example* relates to the history of Christianity in the city of Wolverhampton.[24] Although the Christians of Wolverhampton have inherited a particular image of a "Christian society", the contemporary context in which they live is very different from that in which this inherited model was developed. There is now a feeling of discontinuity, displacement, loss and vulnerability, and the current experience of change is informed by the biblical stories of exile. We have heard this loaded term before. The Christians of Wolverhampton have woven these stories into their own narratives of survival and

---

23 Peter Cruchley-Jones, *Singing the Lord's Song in a Strange Land?*, Frankfurt: P. Lang, 2001.
24 Mark Hathorne, *Building God's City in Wolverhampton: A Study of Local Churches in Mission*, Birmingham PhD thesis, 2004.

come up with four responses to exile. These can be classified as the Remnant, Restoration, Assimilation, and the Pilgrimage models. A remnant community would re-group around a remembered identity; inward looking and past oriented it would make a priority of group survival. The restoration community would add to this the intention of regaining lost ground (mission) and would form alliances in order to recover influence and strength and, if possible, make their view of God predominate in society. A community seeking assimilation, however, would primarily be working outwards and would see God at work in the world outside. Its mission is to "translate" the Christian message and be intelligible and acceptable in a changed historical context. The pilgrim community, finally, is on a journey to God's future. That is, it sees itself, together with others, as being en route to a place where God takes the lead. However, it is important to remember that all these various stories about the loss of the homeland and the search for God's Kingdom are woven into the particular narratives of each community. They are ways of life expressed and embodied in their community's story, and this story is constantly re-told and changed in a manner that is different from any systematic theological discourse. Wolver-hampton's Christians offer us thus a plurality of answers to the question of 'what is God actually doing in Europe?' Taken together, these examples represent a process that can be described as the shifting of the Christian mentality from Christendom to what I have already defined as Christianness: that is, a preparedness to reinterpret one's traditions through vivid interaction with other cultures and religions. This is not so different from the lessons we have already learned from mission history. Social marginality can actually help to ask big questions.

Conclusion

I believe that these two processes of theological learning – the one ecumenical and global, the other local and denominational - are important for the formation of faith in a late-capitalist society such as ours. Both processes help Western Christianity to locate itself: on the one hand, in contradistinction to the prevailing values of mainstream culture; on the other, by evincing a solidarity with the hopes and questions that have been raised from within. These processes are also very important for theological understanding across the continents and cultures. Christians can learn from each other and from others outside their tradition as well. They are not doomed either to a life of spiritual incommunication, or to a state of theological dualism in which faith resides in one place and thought in another. Jenkins' position resurrects an old spectre that was first described by Schleiermacher, namely, that faith would go hand in hand with ignorance, while faithlessness would consort with knowledge.

PAX EUROPA: CRUX EUROPA

Darrell Jackson

1. Europe and the Next Christendom

"Whereas before the collapse of Communism in 1991 there were probably a few thousand Russians and citizens of what is now called the Former Soviet Union living in Britain, there are now at least two hundred thousand, concentrated mostly in London, but also scattered throughout the country. Nowhere has the change been more obvious than at the Cathedral in London. Attendance on Sunday has quadrupled and the social language has changed from English to largely Russian. Similar changes have taken place in Russian communities throughout Western Europe, and in the Romanian and Serbian churches as well.

The face of Europe has changed completely. It has experienced one of the most dramatic peaceful revolutions in history."[1]

This paper is an extended treatment of the themes highlighted in Bishop Basil's 2005 editorial in which he alerts the observant reader to the presence of Christians from countries of the former Soviet Union residing in the UK, the greater majority of them practising an Eastern Orthodox form of Christianity. It is my argument that in his book *The Next Christendom: The coming of Global Christianity*, Philip Jenkins correctly identifies a number of themes that will continue to be of central importance for the Churches and Governments of Europe over coming decades. In his discussion he characterizes Churches of the global South as conservative, mystical, and living with an awareness of 'spiritual force'. He contrasts these with the Churches of the global North which are liberal, secular, and living with reference to a largely rational worldview.

Jenkins' work, of course, is not only addressed to the European context though one suspects that his treatment of Europe, in contrast with that of the African, Asian, and Latin American continents, is not designed to serve merely the cause of Christian mission. Professor

---

1   Sergievo, Bishop Basil of 'One hundred issues and twenty-five years' in *Sourozh* No. 100 May 2005 p1-2

Werner Ustorf argues that the Next Christendom appears to be saying that in order to sustain foreign and domestic policy, the US needs more than oil, it needs a religious vision. The most compelling models for these may now lie in the south. Simultaneously, it is suggested that the US can no longer rely on the continent of Europe because it no longer offers a satisfactory model for Capitol Hill advisers. Part of Europe will become Muslim, a large part is rapidly secularizing, and it will contain large ethnic minority populations within which lie internal civilisational fault-lines. The most obvious of the fault-lines is that between the Christian and the Muslim civilizations.[2] This partly addresses the question, 'Why was the book written?'

A view from Europe

It must be noted that I shall offer a response largely from within the European context, within which I am employed as a Researcher for the Conference of European Churches, the Regional Ecumenical Organisation in Europe.[3] Working within this setting forces me to consider two sets of contrasting contexts between which impulses, people, and capital flow. The north-south axis is hugely significant, and we shall remain in Jenkins' debt for this timely reminder; however within Europe it is important not to ignore the significance of the East-West axis. Central and Eastern Europe now have almost fifteen years of post-Soviet experience. The diversity of ways in which countries and Churches have responded offers a unique laboratory for observing the progress of the Christian religion. Of course, time marches on and the climactic events of 1989 following 'Die Wende' remain only as small pieces of brightly painted concrete gathering dust in the attics of Western Europe. In a post 9/11 world the global South and the Islamic worlds naturally attract our attention and Jenkins' book appears more persuasive and timely than passé analyses of post-Gorbachev Europe.

However, I wish to suggest that to fail to capitalize on the opportunities offered by a closer examination of the religious, social, and political realities that lie along an East-West axis ultimately bear

---

2   For this analysis I am indebted to papers presented by Professor Ustorf at the meeting of BIAMS, 28th June – 1st July 2005 'Why Christendom is an unlikely future for World Christianity' Cliff College Publishing: Sheffield, (forthcoming)

3   The Conference of European Churches was established in 1958 as an initiative of the Churches of Europe to overcome the isolation and separation caused by the immediate post-Cold War political and geographical realities. It has 124 member Churches and Denominations, Orthodox and Protestant, and maintains close relationships with the Catholic Bishops' Conference of Europe

upon consideration of the North-South axis. Consequently I am convinced that is absolutely crucial to examine the potential impact of the Eastern Orthodox Church upon developing European politics and ecclesial realities. However, Jenkins singularly fails to offer an adequate account of the Eastern Orthodox Churches in his thesis.

An inadequate treatment of Eastern Orthodoxy

When he does refer to Eastern Churches, Jenkins treatment of Eastern Orthodoxy is disappointing; both historically as well as in his failure to assess its current impact upon his thesis. He devotes two pages to a section on 'The Eastern Churches' where he appears to characterize it as largely Asian and African. A full whole page is taken up with a discussion of the Ethiopian Coptic church.[4] This overlooks the Orthodox countries of Russia, Greece, Albania, Bulgaria, Romania, Ukraine, Belarus, Macedonia, Serbia, and others that are clearly European. Indeed, the better resourced of these Churches are deeply involved in the resurgence of Orthodox mission in Africa, Latin America, and Asia.[5] It may be that Jenkins' focus on global Pentecostalism is responsible for a failure to spot the presence of increasing numbers of Eastern Orthodox Churches in Africa and Asia, in addition to its resurgence in Central and Eastern Europe following the new freedoms gained in the early nineties by the Churches of former Soviet regimes. The revitalisation of the Orthodox Church in Albania since the early 1990s has been described as a 'Resurrection', for example.

It is not immediately clear why Jenkins discusses the Eastern Churches mainly with reference to the Oriental Orthodox Churches (sometimes described as 'monophysite') of Armenia, Ethiopia, and India, for example. Protestant and Roman Catholic Europe is discussed with no sustained reference to Orthodox Europe. There is an almost complete omission of the contribution of Eastern Orthodoxy in its mission and its contribution to European 'nation-building'. There is nothing, for example, in Chapter two on Orthodox mission to the north; an activity that stretches from the eighth century onwards.[6]

---

4   Jenkins, *The Next Christendom*, p18-19
5   See Jackson, DR., 'Contemporary Orthodox Mission' in *Journal of European Baptist Studies* (forthcoming) in which attention is drawn to the Eastern Orthodox practices of miraculous healing and exorcism and how these have received an enthusiastic welcome in African countries.
6   In fact, the Slavic Lands of Slovakia, Slovenia, and Croatia were evangelised from 780AD onwards by missionaries from Rome. By 1000AD Central and Eastern Europe

Ustorf's thesis is helpful in offering an explanation for the omissions and misrepresentations of Orthodoxy. It may simply be that Orthodox evidence is contrary evidence to Jenkins' presentation of Europe as liberal, secular, and rational. We shall return to a more detailed discussion of the evidence below but we will simply declare our view at this point that it is probably far from true that Jenkins has adequately described Europe.

Jenkins' failure to offer an adequate account of Eastern Orthodoxy is the more surprising given the allusions within *The Next Christendom* to Huntington's 'Clash of Civilizations' thesis, within which the Orthodox world is described as one of eight 'civilizations'. Huntington's contested thesis draws upon a description of the socio-political realities that can be observed in a place such as Romania. Here the civilisational fault-line can be observed running through the heart of the country, drawn between the historically Hungarian Reformed lands and the Romanian Orthodox lands. Both 'civilisations' represented in this particular situation adopt a territorial posture, take a religious character, and are located in a country about to accede to membership in the liberal and secular European Union. The regional politics are, not surprisingly, complex! However, this would be to overlook the potential for both Churches to prove to be a positive influence for greater social coherence. Of course, this is far from the current ecumenical realities in Romania, but it is nevertheless important to note the greater capacity of the Churches of Europe, in contrast with those of the US, for genuine ecumenical dialogue and partnership. For the Reformed and Orthodox Churches in Romania there exist, within both the WCC and the CEC, suitable and existing arenas for mutual understanding and dialogue, possible resources for mediation in the event of conflict, and an ongoing search for the true unity of the Church.

What is true for the Churches of Romania is true elsewhere. The Orthodox Churches in Europe make an important and necessary contribution to ecumenical debate and encounter and for the Protestant Churches of Europe there is a growing understanding of, and sense of appreciation for, the ecclesial and liturgical tradition of the Orthodox Church.

---

had been evangelised by missionaries from Constantinople, inspired by Ss. Cyril and Methodius.

2. Jenkins use of statistical and historical evidence

Jenkins' methodology is reasonably transparent; "...so much of this book concerns numbers and focuses on future religious statistics."[7] In the April 2004 edition of IRM, global statistician Todd Johnson charts the geographical location of the centre of gravity of the global Christian population over the last two thousand years. His map, and its trajectory of 'global Christianity's statistical centre of gravity', is compelling in its simplicity (illustrated below).[8] Jenkins thesis is equally compelling in its construction and accumulation of historical and statistical data. The story of historical, vital, and expanding forms of non-Western Christianity is a familiar one for missiologists and their post-graduate students.[9] In respect of this central element of Jenkins' work one suspects that he has few detractors within the missiological constituency. For example, most BIAMS members would concur readily with the following,

"Christian belief worldwide is no longer a projection of whatever is dominant for academic theologians or biblical studies specialists at Berlin, Oxford, the Sorbonne, and Harvard."[10]

The same is true for ecclesial and denominational identities. In some instances the content that designates orthodox Christianity can be difficult to see on first observing some Churches of the South. In yet other instances the formerly dependant 'daughter' Church from the south has turned to the 'parent' Church of the north and demanded greater liturgical, denominational, ethical, or biblical faithfulness. In short, these may be seen as calls for a return to a *more* orthodox form of denominational Christianity.

7   Jenkins, P., *The Next Christendom The coming of Global Christianity* Oxford University Press: Oxford, 2002. p86

8   Johnson, T. & Chung, SY., 'Tracking Global Christianity's Statistical Centre of Gravity, AD33-AD2100' in *International Review of Mission*, Vol. 93, No. 369, April 2004. p167.

9   See, for example; Walls, AF., 'Africa in Christian History – Retrospect and Prospect' in *Journal of African Christian Thought* Vol 1, No 1 Jan 1998, p 2-15. Sanneh, L., *Encountering the West: Christianity and the global cultural process: the African dimension.* Orbis Books: Maryknoll, 1993. Kaplan, S. (Ed), *Indigenous responses to western Christianity.* New York University Press: New York, 1995. Walls, AF, *The cross-cultural process in Christian history: studies in the transmission and appropriation of faith*, T&T Clark: Edinburgh 2002. Irvin, DT. & Sunquist, SW., *History of the world Christian movement.* Orbis Books: Maryknoll, 2001

10 Yarborough, R. 'The Last and Next Christendom: Implications for Interpreting the Bible' in *Themelios* Vol. 29 No. 1, Autumn 2003. p37

One can point to statistical assumptions made by Jenkins that long-standing researchers in the field have addressed differently but this would be to seek to unnecessarily avoid the weight of the cumulative evidence summarised by Jenkins.[11] Jenkins seems to stress throughout the book that global influence correlates directly to population and ecclesial membership statistics; an analysis that demographics equals power. Though this is certainly contestable,[12] it does not seem adequate to merely point, as does Martin Conway in the pre-Conference email discussions, to the observation of a Kenyan theologian who suggests that whilst there may be large numbers of people attending church services in Kenya, it is difficult to weigh the quality of the faith they believe and are acting by. If one follows Jenkins' analysis carefully, these are *precisely* the conditions that tend to result in Church-State alliances that have characterized Christendom and which will potentially characterize the Next Christendom.

3. Is Europe a thoroughly post-Christendom continent?

As a Baptist missiologist with Anabaptist sympathies I adopt a critical stance towards Christendom. It is now a safe stance to adopt, in something of a contrast with the experience of Anabaptist and Mennonite pioneers who were persecuted for their anti-Christendom convictions from the sixteenth century onwards. However, within mainline Christianity, the possibility of alternative forms of Christianity other than Christendom has a more recent heritage. In 1956, George Macleod, founder of the Iona Community, could write, "...the whole concept of "Christendom" has gone."[13] Macleod's usage is reasonably strong evidence for at least a fifty year career for the notion of 'post-Christendom' and John Howard Yoder suggests that its origins lie, slightly earlier, in the Continental theologies of Barth and his contemporaries in the 1920s.

"In the very broadest sense, the original scandalous outbreak of the 'Theology of the Word' in the 1920s, represented in legend by

---

11   Jenkins criticizes David Barrett of underestimating the strength of Christianity in Africa in 1200 for example. Barrett is normally criticized within the Christian research community for over-estimating! However, Jenkins offers no source for his own estimations.
12   It may equally be argued that larger Christian populations in the South simply offer a larger resource to be exploited on the globalised religious marketplaces where the larger and more powerful Churches of the North still control many of the mechanisms of the market.
13   Macleod, GF., *Only One Way Left* The Iona Community: Glasgow, 1956, p2

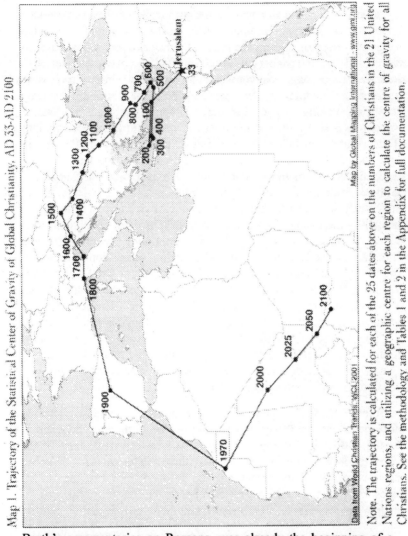

Map 1. Trajectory of the Statistical Center of Gravity of Global Christianity, AD 33-AD 2100

Data from World Christian Trends, WCE 2001

Map by Global Mapping International, www.gmi.org

Note. The trajectory is calculated for each of the 25 dates above on the numbers of Christians in the 21 United Nations regions, and utilizing a geographic centre for each region to calculate the centre of gravity for all Christians. See the methodology and Tables 1 and 2 in the Appendix for full documentation.

Barth's commentaries on Romans, was already the beginning of a post-Christendom reconstruction. So the entire wave of new beginnings that began in German Protestant theology in the 1920s was in one sense the beginning of post-Christendom theology."[14]

---

14 Yoder, JH., 'Karl Barth, post-Christendom theologian' Unpublished paper presented to the Karl Barth Society: Elmhurst IL, June 8, 1995

However, working alongside colleagues from the Eastern Orthodox Church is a salutary reminder that 'post-Christendom' does not accurately describe significant parts of Europe where Constantine is still considered to have been a 'good thing'. It is not enough merely to describe Europe as a post-Christendom continent. In reality it is so much more complex when one considers the Orthodox-majority European nations. The European Union's embrace of Eastern Orthodoxy is so far limited to Greece, Cyprus and the representations of the Ecumenical Patriarch but if further enlargement in 2007 is still set to include Romania and Bulgaria, the number of Orthodox-majority European Union member states will have increased to four. The political processes of the European Union assume a secular basis for Government but with further enlargement eastwards we may anticipate the call by the Roman Catholic Church for a broader discussion of the EU as a community of values being supported by the Orthodox Churches as a reflection of their understanding of mission to society.[15] The formal separation of Church and State in Orthodox EU countries will not deter the Orthodox Churches of these countries from using what influence they have to shape EU policy, just as they use it to influence national policy-making at present in Romania and Bulgaria.

> "The demise of Christendom in Western Europe may not mean the end of Christendom. In post-Communist Eastern Europe, a new Christendom is emerging, with demands for national churches with monopoly positions."[16]

Stuart Murray's perceptive comments accurately describe movements that one may observe within the Orthodox Churches of Central and Eastern Europe as well as, to a lesser extent, some of the other majority Churches also located there. This appears to be an integral component in the cultural and political revival of the nation-states of Central and Eastern Europe, emerging from decades of myopic Soviet misrule. Religious identity, as a central part of cultural

---

<http:www.nd.edu/~theo/research/jhy_2/writings/philsystheo/barth.htm> accessed 24.06.2005

15 Indeed, the General Secretary of the WCC, the Revd Sam Kobia, in initial discussions with the Roman Catholic Pope, Benedict XVI, and the Russian Patriarch, Aleksii II, highlighted the need for a Christian contribution to the discussion of values in Europe. See Zolotov, A., 'WCC's Kobia finds Russian Orthodox visit 'easier' than predecessor' in *Ecumenical News International*, 24 June 2005, and Sandri L., 'Pope Benedict and WCC head support Europe's Christian roots' in *Ecumenical News International*, 24 June 2005

16 Murray, S., *Post-Christendom* Paternoster: Carlisle. 2004 p187

identity, is a potent factor in the task and can be readily seen in countries across the region.

Albania is an interesting example. In 1967 former President, Enver Hoxher, declared Albania to be the world's first atheistic State and worked systematically to uproot religious belief from Albanian society.[17] Today, a newly emergent and revived national Orthodox Church is building roads, schools, and other public facilities. One is left wondering how the Albanian Government will relate to the Orthodox Church; whether grateful civil authorities will be tempted to reward the Orthodox Church with special national status.

Albania is also noteworthy for the careful and sensitive stance of its Archbishop, Anastasias, towards inter-faith dialogue and relationships. He has chosen to champion this method over and against the escalation of inter-religious conflict with the Muslim communities of Albania. It is possible to imagine that, within Europe, resurgent forms of Christianity need not necessarily generate increased conflict with Islamic communities although, of course, this continues to be an issue for the resolution of issues in the Balkans and the accession of Turkey to the EU. In the case of Turkey, a particular question is the manner in which its Government either chooses or refuses to deal with a history of genocide against its indigenous Christian communities.

Lamin Sanneh, commenting on forms of non-Western Christianity takes a slightly more optimistic view than Jenkins. He suggests that religious resurgence threatens liberal, democratic institutions and the assumptions of capitalism and the free market far more than it threatens other religious groups. Resurgent non-Western Christianity has resources other than those of the Enlightenment and Christendom to call upon.[18] If Sanneh is correct, we may anticipate places within Europe where, for the obvious reason that Christianity is enjoying a resurgence at a time when Christendom assumptions are simultaneously held with growing suspicion, a resurgent Church is able to abandon Christendom assumptions and instincts. This, of course, is of huge significance for the future of Christian-Muslim relationships within Europe.

---

17 The story of the Albanian Church is told by Jim Forest in *The Resurrection of the Church in Albania* WCC publications: Geneva 2002

18 See Sanneh, L., *Whose religion is Christianity? The Gospel beyond the West*, Eerdmans: Grand Rapids, 2004

4. Alternative visions of primal Christianity?

Jenkins is close to an overly romanticised view of southern Christianity which he imagines to be closer to ancient forms of Christianity than those that now exist in the north (inevitably portrayed as liberal, rationalistic, and secular). Certainly it is true that many of the Churches of the global south, particularly the African Independent Churches and the Pentecostal churches understand their Churches to be rediscovering a biblical primacy that the Churches of the global north are alleged to have left behind with the Enlightenment. However, Jenkins' treatment fails to acknowledge the absence of a European-style Enlightenment or Reformation within Eastern Orthodoxy.[19] The liturgical and ecclesial tradition of the Orthodox Churches is centuries old, mystical, spiritual, and claims the biblical text as authoritative within the tradition of the Church that was entrusted with the task of its canonical transmission. To imagine oneself to be closer to ancient forms of Christianity is clearly a slightly fraught exercise of historical deconstruction and reconstruction.

It is interesting to note that although some parts of the Christian Church may be ready to concede that the self-understanding and practices of the African Independent Churches are close to ancient forms of Christianity, the Eastern Orthodox Churches are less generous in their assessment. This is especially ironic given that of all the Churches, the Orthodox Churches have probably the most enduring and long-standing claims to being the closest to primal Christianity.

The conservative liturgical and ecclesial practices of the Orthodox Churches locate them far from the Western liberal, secular, and rational Christian orthodoxy which Jenkins argues is in demise. The Eastern Orthodox Churches are far from being 'liberal' and may be considered to be enjoying something of a resurgence of interest and attendance, as noted by Bishop Basil in the opening lines of this paper. However, the Orthodox growth and vitality that can be observed in Europe is typified by large numbers of recent Russian immigrants who far outnumber the original émigrés of the early twentieth century. What may be in evidence among these migrant populations from Central and Eastern European is a tendency to use Church attendance

---

19 Indeed it has been said by Orthodox commentators that the Western tradition uses the term 'enlightenment' to describe an individual exercising rational self-control in opposition to the control of the religious establishment, whilst Eastern Christianity uses it to describe a spiritually advanced member of the Church.

as a means of identity maintenance, at least among the first generation of immigrants.

The European Values Survey and surveys conducted by the Russian Orthodox Church indicate that in Russia there is a higher percentage of the Russian population that considers itself 'Orthodox' than the percentage of people who claim to believe in God. These statistics suggest an adherence to cultural forms of Orthodoxy rather than regular and authentic Orthodox practice and belief. Despite these patterns the Eastern Orthodox Churches continue to attract new converts through programmes of evangelization and re-evangelisation, centred on building places of worship across Europe where Orthodox Liturgy can be celebrated in its ancient and mystical forms. In many of these new places of worship the languages of the Liturgy are far from contemporary. Liturgy is celebrated in ancient linguistic forms; including Slavonic, ancient Greek, Syriac, and Armenian. These present realities reflect the ancient forms of national Christianity that emerged in places such as Armenia and Georgia from the fourth century onwards.

In part, it is possible to understand resurgent forms of Orthodox religious practice as a response to encroaching and oppressive forms of western civilization and secularization that, coupled with the expanding global marketplace of goods and labour, threaten traditional patterns of life. The opposition of ancient and orthodox with contemporary and heterodox is not merely a feature of the contrast of Northern with Southern Christianity, it is also a feature of the contrast of Western with Eastern Christianity.

5. Islam in Europe

Jenkins' argues that both Islam and Christianity, 'have potent traditions of seeking to implement their views through political action.'[20] This is a central part of his treatment of the relationship of Islam with Christianity and this is no surprise given the 'Christendom' hermeneutic that he uses to 'read' the respective religious communities. At the same time he is careful, and correct, to point to examples of peaceful co-existence between the two religious communities. Of all the Christian Churches, the Eastern and Oriental Orthodox have the longest experience of living alongside Muslim

---

20   Jenkins, *The Next Christendom*, p169

neighbours; no other Church has this same experience to draw upon in its current encounter with Islam.[21] It would require careful historical analysis to reveal whether the examples of peaceful co-existence correspond with Jenkins' proposed scenario that conflict between the two 'religious giants' is most likely when a nation has either a Christian or a Muslim minority of 10-20%, sufficient to sustain military struggle and resist religious assimilation by the majority. He further buttresses his case with evidence of higher than average birth rates among immigrant populations than among 'old-stock' populations. The consequence of rapidly increasing migrant communities reaching the 10-20% threshold plays to the strengths of Jenkins' scenario.

However, there are a number of questionable elements in Jenkins' assumptions. He argues that,

> 'since poorer or immigrant groups have higher birth rates than
> the better-off, their religious and cultural traditions become more
> influential over time, a trend that in the worst case could lead to
> instability.'[22]

This seems to overlook the evidence that where migrant communities have become more economically successful it is possible to discern signs of their becoming increasingly secular in outlook.[23] In failing to address economic development within migrant communities, Jenkins also fails to adequately acknowledge that economically successful migrant communities tend to display falling birth rates too. High birth rates are not exclusively explained by religious factors; instanced, for example, by comparing the historical birth rates in Roman Catholic Ireland with those of today. The predictive variables are as likely to be economic as religious.

Other factors that bear upon the discussion at this point also include the gradual assimilation by (or, admittedly, radical rejection of) host cultures by the second and third generations. The comfortable nature of life in the West is preferable to many younger Hindus and Muslims

---

21 Orthodox missiologists point to the need for a vital Orthodox mission in order for there to be an effective Christianisation of Europe, including its Islamic inhabitants. This is reflected in the policy of a small number of Western mission agencies who recognize the need to co-operate with existing Orthodox agencies and Churches in order to touch the lives of Muslims living in Europe and in other parts of the former Soviet Union.
22 Jenkins *The Next Christendom* p167
23 Hitching, B., *McDonalds Minarets and Modernity*, Spear: Sevenoaks, 1996

than is the traditional life their parents and grandparents left behind in either India or Bangladesh.

Also worth noting are the reform-minded scholars from the Islamic world who have embraced a wholly secular outlook but who, in the aftermath of the events of September 11th 2001, have chosen to re-engage with the Islam of their youth in order to stimulate reform movements leading to greater openness and tolerance of 'the other' within Islam.

Reform movements within Islam can be paralleled by those within Orthodoxy. For example, Greek Orthodox theologian Dr Petros Vassiliadis, draws upon elements of the Orthodox tradition and notes that,
> "the Orthodox East, in comparison with the West, is better able to respond positively to the demands for a Christian-Muslim dialogue, partly because of the more advanced pneumatology of its theology."[24]

There is clearly a deep divide between the aspirations of these sentiments and the reality of much Orthodox-Islamic conflict, yet the fact remains that both religious traditions contain the theological resources to facilitate a journey of mutual discovery and trust. As they have begun to take a more confident stance within the European Christian context, Eastern Orthodox and non-Western Churches have been encouraged to re-evaluate their historical perspectives on issues of inter-religious relationships and to do so within the context of ecumenical encounter. Movement towards conciliatory responses can be seen among those Orthodox and non-western Churches who are most ecumenically committed.

I sat in the side hall of the Lutheran parish of Råslett in southern Sweden in February of 2005. With me were a small group of Lutheran parish workers and their priest and the Board and priest of the local Syrian Orthodox Community. They had a decade-long experience of sharing the same building for Sunday worship. Once a year they concelebrated the Eucharist. There were many instances of parish workers managing to secure welfare rights for Syrian immigrants. It was an inspiring visit

---

24 Vassiliadis, P., 'Orthodoxy and Islam' in *Eucharist and Witness* WCC: Geneva 1998 p99
    A similarly fruitful pneumatological approach is evident in the work of Pentecostal
    theologians of religion.

and very worthwhile. However, I was interested to hear a little bit about their respective experiences of Islam. The Swedish pastor started carefully. She spoke about the ministry of the parish being offered to everybody living within it, irrespective of their status within the Church of Sweden, whether baptized or not. She talked about the many immigrants from the Islamic community who had benefited from the parish work, just as had the Syrian Orthodox community. She underlined the characteristic Swedish commitment to tolerance, religious freedom and human rights with an appeal to the Gospel imperative towards love and care for the 'other'. The Syrian priest answered somewhat differently. He spoke of fierce oppression of his peoples in Turkey, Syria, Iran, and Iraq, all Muslim countries. He cautioned gently against too naïve an approach by his Swedish friends. He pointed to the totalitarian tendencies of Islamic states and the close integration of religion and political life within Islamic teaching. He concluded with an appeal to the Gospel imperative to bear witness to Jesus, his teaching and his lifestyle.

My reflection to the discussion was to point to the need for the Swedish Church to help the Syrian community understand the diverse and developing nature of Islam in the West (experiencing its own secularizing pressures and attempting to meet internal and external demands for reform). Secondly, I encouraged them to consider how the Syrian congregation might help the Swedish congregation to better understand non-Western expressions of Islam and thus be better equipped to meet and understand it in its more 'radicalized' forms.

The insights of both Eastern and Western Christians are needed for Europe to better understand Islam and frame a more effective and coherent response to it. The Eastern Orthodox experience of co-existence with Islam is not a wholly successful experience; there are many examples of ethnic and religious conflict. But this is definitely not the only history that can be drawn upon for resources and examples in the current European context, as I hope this section has demonstrated.[25]

---

25 It is also worth noting that Jenkins singles out the Ethiopian Coptic Church for special attention and a certain element of praise. However, former missionary to Ethiopia, Dr.

6. 'Spiritual force'

Jenkins' fascination with Southern Christianity includes those elements that demonstrate the immediacy of God's mystical presence in worship as well as in the daily routine of life: exorcism as a means to deal with demon possession, imploring the Holy Spirit to heal and effect miracles, and interceding for all that is required for the individual believer to experience the full blessing of God upon a victorious Christian life. He puts it succinctly,

> "A key dividing issue for North-South churches is 'spiritual force' and its effects on everyday life."[26]

Had Jenkins taken the Eastern Orthodox Churches into consideration he might have noticed that the greater majority of the Orthodox faithful believe in prayer for miracles, visit shrines because they believe them to be efficacious, and have a high regard for exorcism and divine healing, each of which retains its respective liturgical tradition with the Orthodox. I have attended worship at more than a few Pentecostal and charismatic events and have always encountered in these settings a very high expectation that God would intervene there and then to bless each of us with a miracle. It is the sense of immediacy of God in the worship of the Orthodox Church that underpins the Orthodox claim to having a strongly developed pneumatology. In St. Petersburg, Russia, I had to think very carefully before responding to an innocent question from an Orthodox catechumen, "Do Baptists believe in miracles?" I was tempted to answer, "Yes! But only in Baptist miracles!" Of course, Orthodoxy gives a central place to the miraculous. Later the same week my wife and I were taken by an intelligent, young, Russian, female and Oxford postgraduate to visit the Shrine of St. Xenia. She assured us, with total conviction, that requesting St. Xenia to intercede on her behalf was the most effective way of securing health, a husband, and a home.

The Group for Evangelisation of Churches Together in England hosted a consultation on 'Evangelising Contemporary Spirituality'

Peter Cotterell suggests that a more engaged missionary vision by the Ethiopian Church in the fifth and sixth centuries might just have stimulated a mission to the Arabs of the middle East that might possibly have diminished the impact of Qur'anic forms of monotheism. Orthodox scholars occasionally express regret for the historical failure of the Orthodox Churches of the Middle East to develop an effective mission to their Arab neighbours.

26   Jenkins, *The Next Christendom*, p123

during June 2005. The worship was 'holistic', multi-sensory, participative, and meditative. It drew upon 'ancient' and esoteric spiritual sources to inform its shape. Several of the images were taken from posters that are for sale in many so-called 'New Age' stores. As Europe's churches look Eastwards for inspiration in reaching post-Christian citizens tired of sterile, overly-intellectual, reductionist worship, it is likely that Eastern, traditional Orthodox spirituality will be considered as an alternative reference point to Eastern, esoteric spirituality for enriching contemporary spirituality in the West.

If Jenkins is right in his assessment that spiritual force is a key dividing issue then we are again forced to conclude that only by omitting reference to the Orthodox Churches and their contribution to European Christianity is it possible for Jenkins to conclude that the churches of the North are rational, secular, and liberal.

7. 'Rational, liberal and secularised' churches and their relationship with Orthodoxy through the WCC and CEC

In their increasing frustration with the ecumenical movement, the Orthodox Churches in the early 1990s began to agitate for a means of engagement that was more authentically 'Orthodox'. They were critical of what they perceived to be an 'unspiritual' business style that relied upon majority voting (that always favoured the majority Protestant membership of the Council) and business procedures that were typically Anglo-German. The 1991 Canberra WCC Assembly offered two contrasting approaches to the theme, 'Come Holy Spirit!' with the Orthodox taking exception to the presentation by South Korean theologian Chung Hyun-Kyung. The ensuing Orthodox Canberra-Chambésy document redefined the priorities of the WCC. It ultimately contributed to the consensus method for conducting business and voting at meetings of the World Council of Churches; finally adopted in 2004 and then used for the first time by the Central Committee in 2005.

The current frustrations of the Eastern Orthodox are focussed closely on questions of mission, evangelisation, and proselytism. For example, the Conference of European Churches has been urged to take this matter into its Research in European Mission and Evangelism programme and initial results are expected by the end of 2006. The Orthodox have secured several important joint statements concerning proselytism within the WCC and CEC but there remains the suspicion that their complaints are still not being taken seriously. They point to continuing examples where even member churches of the CEC or the WCC can be considered guilty of proselytism. More considered Orthodox observers offer several key critiques of official ecumenical policy as it reflects the intricate inter-relationships and issues raised by the interaction of new and traditional Churches from East and West, North and South.

Vassiliadis suggests that,

> "the revival of proselytism by certain evangelical groups outside, but also within, the WCC is not so much the result of historical circumstances (such as the collapse of totalitarian regimes, in particular in Central and Eastern Europe) as it is a conscious reaction to the 'openness' of the church to the outside world, especially after the latest developments in the ecumenical movement..."[27]

Other voices have also being raised within the WCC, especially from within the Conference for World Mission and Evangelism, that the fuller participation of the newer and Pentecostal Churches of the south in the WCC should be encouraged. Orthodox critics charge that the failure of the WCC to do so merely maintains the current unhappy situation that prevails with regards to proselytism by Churches and groups uncommitted to ecumenical encounter. Joint statements and processes can only have effect among those who sign them.

Of course, we should not remain insensitive to Murray's claim that resurgent Christendom versions of Churches in the East will tend to want to restrict what they perceive to be counter-mission within their respective territories. With Europe located at the intersection of the North-South and East-West axes, these issues will become ever more sensitive as the Churches of the South establish congregations in the territories considered to belong to the historic Churches of the North. Set against current discussions of mission and proselytism these issues take on a heightened urgency with the renewed prospect of suspicion, misunderstanding and potential conflict.

The 2005 WCC Conference for World Mission and Evangelism for the first time included full participants from the Roman Catholic Churches and the Pentecostal and Evangelical Churches. Their

---

27 Vassiliadis, P., *Eucharist and Witness*, p33

inclusion has to be seen as hopeful. At the CWME conference, Orthodox, Protestant, and Roman Catholic healing rites from both the global south and north were offered as part of the main programme. Pentecostal-Orthodox dialogue was featured at one of the Conference's Synaxeis (or workshop). The global engagement of Orthodoxy and newer forms of the Christian church from the south within the ecumenical and pan-evangelical movements and organisations is likely to lead to a form of renewal within the traditional churches of the north. It is naturally somewhat difficult to predict the nature of this renewal, but the early signs are reasonably encouraging and suggest that the ecumenical journey is far from over.

8. Secular Europe?

Following the Soviet collapse of 1989-90, European Union enlargement (as an example of one 'European project') has propelled many of the Central and Eastern European countries in the direction of new political and social realities. At the same time, worldwide ecumenical interest is shifting to the churches of the global south for very understandable reasons. There may be many reasons why it seems that the Churches of Central and Eastern Europe are not that interesting any more. However, this region probably needs even greater care and attention than it did before the changes. Growing nationalism, the question of minority groups, and sensitivities between Eastern Orthodox and the other Christian Churches remain. A somewhat cursory glance at an initial range of issues suggests the need for greater East-West cooperation relevant to the everyday challenges of mission in societies undergoing rapid transition.

Resurgent religiosity and spirituality

Despite the cautions suggested by the findings of the European Values Survey[28], the trends across Europe should make sobering reading for leaders of the European Churches that are seen to have decreasing relevance to the everyday lives of Europe's citizens. However, as I have travelled I have begun to feel that a more nuanced understanding of secularisation and its impacts may be called for. In their work *Religion in Secularizing Europe*, summarising the findings of the European Values Surveys of 1980, 1990, and 1998 the report's

---

28 Religiosity in Iceland is surprisingly higher than in all Northern European Countries, Poland and Ireland are far less affected by secularization and individualism than other countries. In Spain, levels of trust in the Church are increasing and in Italy, religiosity is increasing (though not institutional religious activity).

editors write,

"Secularization has not proceeded at a similar pace all over Europe."[29]

For many citizens of Central and Eastern Europe, 'doubly secularised' may be a more appropriate description. For them, Soviet atheistic materialism has been followed rapidly by western, capitalistic form of materialism. The story of Gabor is instructive in this regard:

Gabor Kovacs is a bright, engaging and articulate Hungarian in his mid 30s.

He is English and German-speaking and learnt English in his spare time to enable him to improve his career prospects with the multi-national companies that have been relocating offices to Budapest over the last fifteen years or so. He has worked for various multi-national offices in Budapest over the last seven or eight years and although he recognises the economic advantage of working for the western multi-nationals, he is very aware of the social cost to the individual employees and feels this personally. He speaks of being a 'slave' of western multi-nationals and complains that the higher than average salary brings with it a higher than average set of expectations. He laments that he is unable to give more time to his family commitments. He complains that colleagues in London, Paris, or Frankfurt have high unrealistic expectations. He suspects that they sometimes tell him that his allotted tasks should only need eight hours in the working day when in fact they know that eleven are needed. His working day is typically eight to eleven hours long, a fact he resents.

He readily suggests that the Soviet education of his youth offered no religious education but reveals that he is very interested in religion as an alternative to capitalism's inhuman processes. He thinks that it might provide a way of achieving inner peace, harmony and a way of dealing with stresses of modern life. He also wonders whether religion can provide an alternative ideological or value base.

He suggests that Hungary and other EU accession states are likely to pay a high social cost for entry into the EU and believes

---

29   Halman, L. & Riis, O., *Religion in Secularizing Society* (Brill: Leiden, 2003), p9

that many of the accession states are in the pockets of the larger Western nations. Perhaps somewhat ironically therefore, he aspires to be a world citizen, or at least a European one (although he hesitates to tie this too closely to the European Union), and enjoys travelling. He is fearful of nationalisms and is fearful that such factors may be de-stabilising in the enlarged EU. He asks whether the EU knows what it is doing by inviting potentially unstable nations into enlarged membership.

His interest in religion extends particularly to eastern, esoteric, religions, including Buddhism. He readily admits that he has little time for the study and devotion required by most religions. His understanding of religion is fairly individualistic and he rarely talks of religious 'groups', 'communities', or even 'churches'.

My encounter with Gabor reveals, I believe, that there are Europeans who, though carrying the burden of double-secularisation, instinctively believe that religious belief may in some way provide a way towards deeper personal integration and possibly a way to resist the de-humanising tendencies of the western multi-nationals that have recently arrived in Central and Eastern Europe.

Such an instinctive response underlines the strength of the sound-bite that, "Secularity may have won all the arguments but religion still gets the votes."[30] The scientific methodology of secular societies is clearly concerned with providing answers yet it clearly fails to provide answers to personal choices such as, 'What should I spend my money on?' or, 'What life choices am I to make?' In short, science may not be answering the questions we care about.

Metropolitan Daniel of Romania, suggests that in the face of such a predicament,

"Secularization obliges the Church to renew its spiritual life, to become more responsible in the world, more sensitive to the presence of Christ in the "signs of the time", in the social struggle for justice, freedom and human dignity; even to experience often the situation of being marginalized, in order to better understand those who are marginalized or forgotten in

---

30 Sommerville, JC. 'Post-Secularism marginalizes the University' in *Church History,* 71:4 (December 2002) p.848

different societies. Secularization calls paradoxically for more holiness of life, for a deeper spirituality."[31]

Resisting the de-humanising tendencies of the western institutions and corporations, in some instances, is given institutional expression. In countries such as Russia, for example, the Orthodox Church can be understood as an important ally in resisting the inroads being made by less desirable elements of western individualism and secularization (although in some versions, this seems to give way to extreme ideological expressions). In such countries, perhaps ironically, where minority churches feel themselves disadvantaged by the dominance of a majority Church, the attraction of a secular State as the only apparent means of securing religious freedoms is difficult to resist.

I wish to argue that Europe is far from the secular continent that Jenkins assumes it to be, if by 'secular' we mean the widespread phenomena of individuals who live their lives with no reference to religiosity or spirituality. The evidence of a 'return to the religious' is not lacking. Resurgent Orthodoxy offers one such piece of evidence alongside the stubborn statistics that indicate belief in God, the practice of prayer, belief in life after death, and many other indicators of religious belief. To quote the European Values Survey findings,

"'All age groups show increasing levels of general religiosity when they get older, but as soon as institutional aspects are evaluated, all age groups show declining levels of religiosity. There is indeed an institutional crisis, but not necessarily a religious crisis'[32]

It is the institutional crisis that is naturally of most concern to ecclesiastical and political leaders of Europe, for religious institutions are usually the stewards of religious vision. The same might be said of political institutions undergoing a corresponding crisis. If Jenkins is correct to imply that States require a religious vision, the European religious vision of the future might well have become so diverse and detached from its institutional foundations that it works against the attempt to create a unifying vision for Europe's political institution and machinery. This is the same question raised by the omission of a reference to 'God' in the Preamble to the draft Constitution of the

---

31 Metropolitan Daniel Ciobotea *Confessing the Truth in Love: Orthodox perceptions of life, mission and unity* (Iasi: Trinitas, 2001)
32 Halman, L. & Riis, O., *Religion in Secularizing Society*, Brill: Leiden, 2003 p11

European Union. However, to imply that religiosity and spirituality are absent from Europe is far from the case and susceptible to the changing tide of religious affectation or a re-energised Christian mission, Orthodox, Protestant, and Roman Catholic.

9. Concluding comments

This paper has demonstrated the relative lack of attention to the Eastern Orthodox Churches within 'The Next Christendom' thesis of Philip Jenkins. Consequently his analysis lacks the necessary nuances as it bears upon 'Europe', current and historical. This is a particularly significant omission given the role played within his thesis of different Christendom conceptions of Christianity. Without giving proper attention to the role of Eastern Orthodoxy within Europe one simply struggles to portray Europe as a continent within which Christendom models of the Church co-exist with post-Christendom and, possibly, pre-Christendom models. It has been suggested that Orthodoxy demonstrates subtle accommodations through its engagement with the Ecumenical movement at a number of junctures. These illustrate a range of suggestive possibilities illustrating Europe's capacity to integrate, assimilate, and even subvert the alternative visions of global Christianity that accompany the migration of peoples from the global south and east.

Ultimately a less than adequate account of the Orthodox Churches within Europe undermines Jenkins' thesis that 'northern' or 'western' Christianity stands in marked contrast with the churches of the south or east. The Orthodox Churches of Europe have been shown to exhibit all of the characteristics that Jenkins finds in the churches of the south. Further, the evidence we have offered is widespread within and central to Orthodox dogma. Consequently we are not persuaded that Jenkins characterizations, nor his thesis, adequately explain European religious complexity and diversity.

NON-WHITE PENTECOSTALISM ON A WHITE CONTINENT: MISSIOLOGICAL CHALLENGES FROM AFRICA FOR EUROPE

Valentin Dedji

Understanding the Typology of Pentecostal, Charismatic and AICs[1]

In entering this research field, I quickly realise as Allan Anderson did before me, that one of the fundamental problems in the academic study of Pentecostalism has been 'a misinformed interpretation of Pentecostal and Charismatic history and theology, where the role players are mainly white north-Americans and western Europeans'.[2] In this paper, I will challenge this interpretation. I will restore the credentials of some non-white indigenous initiators who, not only played a pioneering role in establishing the Pentecostal movement locally, but also contributed to a new dynamism that spread Pentecostalism world-wide. This will highlight aspects of black origins of Pentecostalism. According to MacRobert, 'The particular attraction of Pentecostalism in non-Western societies lies in its black experiential roots which provide a substratum of enduring values and themes for the bulk of the movement outside of white north America and Europe.'[3] MacRobert goes on to stress that Pentecostalism has largely been coloured by a distinctively black culture thus producing a black form of Christianity. Likewise, in giving his evidence on the black origins of Pentecostalism in North America, Albert Raboteau

---

1. The acronym AIC is used to represent terms such as, African Independent Churches; African Instituted Churches; African Indigenous Churches; African Initiated Churches and African Initiatives in Christianity. African Independent Churches or African Indigenous Churches are preferred in this paper mainly because of the posture the AICs adopted as independent of Western European missionaries and the argument that they represent real 'authentic' African churches that are not coloured by Western European missionary ecclesiology.
2. Allan Anderson, *An Introduction to Pentecostalism* (Cambridge: Cambridge University Press, 2004), p.15.
3. Ian MacRobert, 'The Black Roots of Pentecostalism' in Jan A.B. Jongeneel, a.o (eds.), *Pentecost, Mission and Ecumenism: Essays on Intercultural Theology* (Frankfurt am Main: Peterlang, 1992), p.77.

asserts that:

> Shaped and modified by a new environment, elements of African folklore, music, language, and religion were transplanted to the New World by the African diaspora ... African styles of worship, forms of ritual, systems of belief, and fundamental perspectives have remained vital on this side of the Atlantic, not because they were preserved in a 'pure' orthodoxy but because they were transformed. Adaptability, based upon respect for spiritual power wherever it originated, accounted for the openness of African religions to other religious traditions and for the continuity of a distinctively African religious consciousness.[4]

In general, Pentecostal and Charismatic movements have many different shapes and sizes all over the world. Therefore, it is very difficult to find some common unifying features or distinctiveness by which they might be defined. Johnstone and Mandryk define 'Charismatics' as 'those who testify to a renewing experience of the Holy Spirit and present exercise of the gifts of the Spirit'. As for 'Pentecostals', they are defined as 'those affiliated to specifically Pentecostal denominations committed to a Pentecostal theology usually including a post-conversion experience of a baptism in the Spirit'.[5]

Given the diversity and complexity of the religious scene in Africa, any attempt at defining the characteristics of Pentecostal and Charismatic churches in Africa becomes even more difficult. Walter Hollenweger notes that:

> There is no reliable overview of the charismatic renewal in the third world ... problems of establishing the extent of the character of the charismatic renewal are almost insurmountable, first because the scene is changing all the time; secondly, because there is no accepted definition of the charismatic renewal; and thirdly, because it is almost impossible to get accurate statistics and description.[6]

However, as Cephas Omenyo rightly put it, 'phenomenologically and theologically, the AICs can be considered as Pentecostal and

---

4. Albert Raboteau, *Slave Religion: the Visible Institution in the Antebellum South* (Oxford: Oxford University Press, 1978), pp.4-5
5. Patrick Johnstone and Jason Mandryk, *Operation World: 21st Century Edition* (Carlisle, UK: Paternoster Press, 2001), pp. 3, 21, 775, 762.
6. Walter Hollenweger, 'Charismatic Renewal in the Third World: Implications for Mission.', *Occasional Bulletin of Missionary Research*, 4, (1980), pp.68-72.

Charismatic movements.'[7]   The AICs are characterised by faith healing, vibrant worship and full-of-lively African music accompanied largely by African musical instruments. Adherents of the AICs perceive them as providing satisfaction for the African's deep religious and spiritual quest and the search for authentic spirituality and provision of answers to questions emerging from the African worldview.[8]   Most founders and leaders of the AICs were subconsciously seeking to establish churches that had African character, and churches which were radically different from Western mission founded churches. As a result some scholars perceive the AICs as real 'authentic African' churches in view of their ability to help Africans to face a number of challenges that the Western founded churches could not adequately address.[9] This had led H.W. Turner to describe them as churches which have been 'founded in Africa by Africans primarily for Africans'.[10]   This is where Andrew Walls suggests that much of the distinctiveness of African theology lies in the manner in which it formalizes the syntheses produced by countless African Christians as they affirm, deny, suppress, redirect and reinterpret the traditional forms of African religion in light of Christian teaching.[11] Even more clearly, Walls argues that the distinctive nature of African Christianity cannot be understood without reference to what has gone before. There are, following Walls, more continuities than discontinuities, in the fact, for example, that the Christian God in Africa has a vernacular name and in the application of the Christian tradition to already existing maps of the universe. Others see the AICs as protest against the Eurocentric disposition of the mainline churches in Africa.[12]

However, whatever the 'primal vision' of the founders of particular AICs might be, AICs are most of the times meeting points of Western

7. Cephas Omenyo, *Pentecost Outside Pentecostalism* (Zoetermeer , The Netherlands: Boekencentrum Publishing House, 2002), p.93.
8. See J.S. Pobee & Gabriel Ositule II, *African Initiatives in Christianity: The Growth, Gifts and Diversities of Indigenous African Churches: A challenge to the Ecumenical Movement*, Geneva: World Council of Churches Publication, 1998, 10.
9. See, e.g., J.S. Pobee 'Confessing Christ in an African Instituted Churches' in: J.S. Pobee (ed.), *Exploring Afro-Christology*, Frankfurt am Main: Peter Lang, 1992, 145.
10. H.W. Turner, 'A Typology of African Religious Movements', *Journal of Religion in Atica*, 1 (1967), 1.
11. Andrew Walls, 'Introduction: African Christianity in the History of Religions.' In C. Fyfe and A. Walls (eds.), *Christianity in Africa in the 1990s* (Edinburgh, Centre of African Studies, 1996), p.4.
12. See Cephas Omenyo, *Pentecost Outside Pentecostalism*, p.4.

and African elements of theology. The founders and leaders were all members in the already established mainline churches.[13] The significance of this fact is that they had their basic Christian upbringing from the mainline churches. As a result, they merged their ideas of African Christianity with traditions and practices of the Western founded churches from which they broke away. Basically the two traditions share in the use of the same Scriptures except that they differ in their methods of interpretation. It is sometimes possible to guess which mainline tradition an AIC founder or leader came from by studying features of a particular AIC.[14] Among the larger groups of classical AICs can be found the following: the *amaNazareta* of Isaiah Shembe and the Zion Christian Church of Engenas Lekganyane, both in South Africa; Samuel Mutendi's Zion Christian Church and Johane Maranke's African Apostolic Church in Zimbabwe; Alice Lenshina's Lumpa Church in Zambia; Simon Kimbangu's Church of Jesus Christ in the Democratic Republic of Congo; and finally the Cherubim and Seraphim Church; the Church of the Lord (Aladura) and the Celestial Church of Christ in Benin and Nigeria.

According to Daneel (1998), three broad types can be distinguished in the literature. The first includes the Ethiopian type or non-prophetic church movements which emerge as a reaction to the white-led mission churches, though in other respects are very like them. It is these churches, moreover, that embody an 'Ethiopian' or distinctively African ideology - i.e. one that is free from European influence. The second or spirit-type place much greater emphasis on the work of the Holy Spirit, displayed in charismatic forms of worship and prophetic gifts including healing and various forms of exorcism. Daneel includes in this category all Zionists and a wide range of Apostolic churches. Initially there are the Messianic churches (a more controversial category), in which the founder-leader of the church or movement becomes much more central (as a miracle worker or resistance figure, for example), displacing in some senses the centrality of Christ. The controversy surrounds the degree to which the leader obscures the salvific work of Christ.

---

13. See Ione Acquah, *Accra Survey*, London: University Press, 1958, 150.
14. See Cephas Omenyo, 'Mission as Intercultural Theology' in Martha Fredericks a.o. (eds), *Towards an Intercultural Theology*, (Zoetermeer: Meinema, 2003), p.176

Traditional Pentecostalism

The Aladura Movement in Nigeria

According to Allan Anderson, 'Lagos is arguably the most Pentecostal city in the world.'[15] It has a long history of independent African churches emphasizing spiritual gifts, dating back to the time of the great influenza epidemic of 1918. Then, those who left the mission churches and sought God in prayer for healing became known as 'Aladura', a Yoruba word meaning 'possessors of prayer'. The white-robed, often bare-footed Aladura are still found in thriving churches, but in Lagos one cannot fail to notice hundreds of relatively new churches with signboards on every street corner. Pentecostals are everywhere: they preach in buses, at market places and in massive campgrounds, tents, stadiums, churches and auditoriums. They dominate the media. Pentecostalism has profoundly affected all forms of Christianity in Nigeria.

Modern Pentecostalism

As for the picture of modern Pentecostalism in Africa, Paul Gifford quite rightly raises some critical issues regarding their typologies (to what extent are the traditional typologies still applicable?), about 'Africanness', about politics and finally about the connection between Pentecostal movements and Africa's economic collapse. Within this rather daunting list, it is worth pausing for a moment on 'Africanness' in that it raises the problematic distinction between new forms of Pentecostalism and more traditional forms of independency, parts of which have quite rightly been described as Pentecostal.

In what way are these new churches a flowering of African Christianity? What attitude do these new Pentecostal churches adopt towards African Culture? To what extent is this new African Christianity underpinned by an African metaphysic? What is the Western factor in this phenomenon? To what degree are Western missionaries involved? What role does Western literature, technology, media play? To what degree is it Western?[16]

Beneath such questions, the issue of continuity reappears once again and in a particularly complicated form. Harvey Cox (1996), for

---

15. Allan Anderson, *Introduction to Pentecostalism*, p.4
16 . Paul Gifford, *New Dimensions in African Christianity,* (Nairobi, All Africa Conference of Churches, 1992), p.5

example, regards AICs as the African expression of worldwide Pentecostalism. Meyer's work on Ghana, together with Maxwell's own on Zimbabwe, focuses on the relationship between Pentecostalism and modernity itself. Using material from a detailed ethno-graphic study of the Zimbabwe Assemblies of God, Africa (ZAOGA), Maxwell (1998, 1999) addresses two interrelated issues: the prosperity gospel itself and its links to the American Bible Belt. Both are controversial. Maxwell concludes that there is indeed contact between Zimbabwe and the United States in terms of theological justification for the accumulation of wealth, but that Southern African sources and local concerns are paramount for the members of ZAOGA, not least the need to establish ways of surviving in conditions of rapid economic change. In so far as it succeeds in this aim, Pentecostalism in Africa fits well with both the values and the institutions of modernity. The capacity of African Pentecostalism to operate across borders becomes a pivotal theme to which we now turn.

The Periphery in the Centre: African New Religious Movements in Europe

As quite rightly observed by Grace Davie, the impact of African forms of religion in Europe is a relatively new field of enquiry.[17] She goes on to stress that 'it is a subject which many Europeans find provocative in so far as it questions many of their most deep-seated assumptions'. The relationship between Europe and Africa is assumed to operate in a particular direction: its apparent reversal is correspondingly disturbing. For example, in a remarkable piece of work Ter Haar demonstrates how Ghanaian communities understand themselves as evangelists and missionaries in Netherlands (one of the most secular countries in Europe). Drawing on the Old Testament image of' dry bones', members of these churches construct Europe as a spiritual desert to which they are called as evangelists, a fact that is not always appreciated by the host society.

The reversal of responsibilities implied in this attitude drastically overturns the traditional relations between Africans and Europeans. It is in sharp contrast with the conventional view of existing north-south relations, often equated with black-white relations, and hardly conforms to the marginal position of the

---

17 . Grace Davie, *Europe: The Exceptional Case* (London: Darton Longman & Todd Ltd, 2002), p.84.

majority of Africans in Europe. On the European side, this reversal of roles appears difficult to appreciate as it does not comply with the stereotypes often attached to Africa. Africans are traditionally represented as on the receiving end and *Europe* on the giving end of a relationship characterised by unequal transfer. (Ter Haar 1998a: 168).

Caribbean and African immigrations into Britain are relatively well documented; so too the vibrant church life of these communities in many of Britain's larger cities. There are two sides to this story: first the kind of Christianity that immigrant groups brought with them, but second - and crucially - the initial rejection of the migrant Christians by the established denominations in Britain (for the most part in England). The phenomenal growth of black-led churches was the direct consequence of the latter (Gerloff 1992) - congregations which grew first by immigration, then for demographic reasons, but finally by receiving 'converts' from the historic churches. Such churches become, moreover, an indispensable focus for the cultural identity of their communities, the more so given the very difficult economic and social conditions in which these populations are obliged to live.

Denominationally, however, they are extremely diverse. Gerloff (1992), for example, identifies eleven different traditions, by far the largest being the Pentecostals, themselves divided into three families (with sub-groups). The remainder include Methodists, Baptists, Sabbatarians, the Holiness Movements, a significant group of AICs (notably from Nigeria and Ghana) and lastly the British Rastafarian movement.

If the experience in Britain (and more especially England) has been longer than most, that in The Netherlands is recent. The study of African immigrant communities in a number of Dutch cities has become, however, the focus of Ter Haar's work on the African diaspora in Europe. The main focus of this account lies in a developed study of the Ghanaian community in the Bijlmer, a suburb of Amsterdam 15 which becomes de facto an illustration of the wider experience of Africans in Europe.

There are three basic categories of African Christian religious groups in Europe. The first and most popular of these are religious groups which exist as branches or parishes of mother churches with headquarters in Africa. Examples are the Celestial Church of Christ

Worldwide, Church of the Lord-Aladura, the Redeemed Christian Church of God, the Church of Pentecost International, the Kimbanguist Church etc. The second category refers to those groups that started and have their headquarters in Europe, but with intent to establish or open branches in Africa and elsewhere. Examples are the True Teachings of Christ's Temple (Holland), the Christian Outreach Mission Church (Hamburg), the Aladura International Church (London), Victory Ministries (Oberhausen), the Born Again Christ Healing Church (London) etc. Another category is inter-denominational groups or para-church organizations existing as somewhat loose groups (prayer/fellowship) without proper or formalized administrative structures.

Towards an International Vision of African Pentecostalism

One basic characteristic of AICs is their vitality, dynamism and their demonstration of a great capacity for incorporating change, such as that witnessed in contemporary era due to shifts in global migration patterns. One remarkable fall-out of the globalization process is the increasing 'dispersal' of Africans beyond their continental context, thus moving them from a local to a global presence. Consequently, the bridging of gap brought about several strategies through which religious interchanges were exerted on the worldwide religious landscape. Ter Haar (1998: 23) notes that 'their spread overseas has involved those churches in international networks of relations to which they did not have access until the late twentieth century. There is now a two-way channel of communication between churches inside and outside Africa, whether they belong to the first or the second generation of African-initiated churches. This shows that Africa has become fully part of a global world in religious terms. The founding of African independent churches all over the world is a sure sign of this'. This section highlights some of such tendencies towards globalization.

a. Local groups embarking on missionary task to propagate their religious message to the wider world i.e. the Celestial Church of Christ, Church of the Lord - Aladura, Cherubim and Seraphim, the Redeemed Christian Church of God, Winners Chapel, Christ Chapel, the Church of Pentecost etc.

b. Individuals or groups seeking to establish links with like-minded international or overseas religious organizations i.e. Truth and Life

Church, the Apostolic Faith Mission, the Apostolic Church etc. Such relationships are expressed in terms of one or more of the following: symbolism, religious texts (sacred literature), financial aids, missionary presence (personnel), moral religious support, music/language etc.

c. External religious bodies with the intent of sowing their religious ideologies within the African continent i.e. Four Square Gospel Church, the Full Gospel Businessmen Fellowship; the Jehovah Witness, the Church of the New Jerusalem (Swedenborgism), the Unification Church, Christ for all Nations etc.

d. Initiatives of the local groups or diasporan communities towards joining ecumenical links or ties (national/continental/inter-continental) i.e. Organization of African Instituted Churches (OAIC), Partnership of African Christian Communities in Europe (PACCE), Council of African and Caribbean Churches (CACC), World Council of Churches (WCC) etc.

e. The adoption of such labels as 'international', 'worldwide', 'global', 'world' to their nomenclatures thus indicating their religiously inspired and promising access to trans-nationalism and the wide variety of their international linkages. A few examples here arc the Celestial Church of Christ Worldwide, Aladura Church Inter-national, Rhema Churches International, International Central Gospel Church, the Global Revival Outreach, World Miracle Church, the Harvest Ministries International, Church of Pentecost International, Liberty Church International, Praise and Power Gospel International Ministry, Bethel Prayer Ministry International, the Victory Bible Church International, Lighthouse Chapel Church, Gospel Light International Church etc. Some of these groups already have branches/parishes in different parts of Europe and elsewhere in the world while others are seeking to plant branches elsewhere. However, there abound some groups with a sole branch but which already attaches these terms to their names. These portray a great deal their intent to transcend local boundaries to global ones. It was this noticeable global dispersal of these churches that perhaps informs Ter Haar's (1998: 24) suggestion to re-christen them **'African International Churches'**, retaining the old initials AIC but assuming a new, contemporary meaning. She hints that "Most churches in fact label themselves as 'international churches', expressing their aspiration to be part of the international world in which they believe themselves to have a universal task'.

A new feature of some of these churches is the symbolic display of their global operational frameworks through the hoisting of flags (banners) at or near the pulpits as well as within the church vicinity, of each of the countries to which the church has branched out or where there is some form of religious affiliation, or with whom they already established ecumenical relationship.

An Alternative Understanding of Ecclesiology: A Serious Missiological Challenge

While during the last four decades, 'believing without belonging' has become the major fashionable religious tendency in Britain (and in Europe), African communities underline the fact that following Christ includes *belonging*, not just believing.   This has probably been informed by two contradicting cultural concepts: where the French philosopher René Descartes stated: 'I know therefore I am', (*Cogito ergo sum*) Africans would rather say: '*I belong to, therefore, we are'*. This implies that we are created for community, fashioned for fellowship, and formed for a family. Applied to the New Testament' theology, this sheds 'new insights' on Africans' understanding of church membership.   They refer to Paul to whom, being a member of the church meant being a vital organ of a living body, an indispensable, interconnected part of the Body of Christ.   Here appears a serious challenge to European Christians to recover and practice the biblical meaning of church' membership.   The church is a body, not a building; an organism, not an organization.   As such, Africans understand that disconnected and cut off from the lifeblood of a local body, your spiritual life will wither and eventually cease to exist. This is why, the first symptom of spiritual decline is usually inconsistent attendance at worship services and other gatherings of believers.

Conclusion

The international representation of African Pentecostal Churches in Europe from the mid 1980s onwards, shows that 'the global claim' came to feature prominently showing that they are not confined within the limitations of the present nation-state, but that beyond its borders and cultural boundaries, the interpenetration with other cultural contexts is actively sought and given a place in their ideology, organization and religious experience.   Davie is right in suggesting that

'The presence of African Churches in Europe needs to be taken very seriously.'[18] African missions travel along pre-existing social relations such as family, friendship, village or island community, and trade and work comradeship. They rest on charismatic leadership, communicate in songs and signals, and understand the human person in his or her relationship to community. Therefore faith becomes the light, reliable and comforting baggage in the process of migration and crisis.[19] In terms of the religious life of Europe, these congregations have a very particular position. Almost uniquely, they exhibit a dual nature: in terms of their Christianity. They are part of the mainstream, but in terms of their vitality, their distinctive styles of worship and their capacities to disconcert, they exemplify the features of an immigrant community[20]. Hence their undoubted significance in the continuing evolution of Christianity in this part of the world.

18. Grace Davie, *Europe: The Exceptional Case*, p.111
19. 'Editorial', *International Review of Mission, Special issue on the Cambridge Conference: a Milestone in Progress* (2000), 354: 275-80.
20. Grace Davie, *Religion in Modern Europe: A Memory Mutates* (Oxford: Oxford University Press, 2000), p.149.

Part III

GLOBAL
PERSPECTIVES

POST COLONIALISM

Who Can Say What and To/For Whom? Postcolonial Theory and Christian Theology

Vinoth Ramachandra

The Colonial Legacy

It is a remarkable fact that, as recently as the 1930s, eighty-four percent of the earth's surface area was under European colonial rule. Formal decolonisation was a central event of the second half of the twentieth century, and one that has had profound repercussions for societies all over the world, the colonisers as much as the colonised. For instance, much of the menial labour force in British public services today, on which the rest of society depends so heavily, is made up of migrants from former British colonies; and the same holds true for the Netherlands and France. Many of the protracted conflicts in the world today trace their roots to Britain's imperial policies, whether it be Iraq, Palestine, Kashmir, Burma, Zimbabwe or Northern Ireland.

European colonialism not only plundered wealth from the colonies but also violently reshaped physical territories, social terrains, knowledge-systems and human identities. The economies of colonised peoples were restructured and locked into those of Europe so that there was a flow of human and natural resources between colonised and colonial countries. The massive global shifts of population that we have witnessed in the past fifty years were anticipated by movements of both colonised and coloniser from the eighteenth century onwards. Just as opium was transported to China from India by the English East India Company and exchanged for tea that was then shipped to England, slaves were moved from Africa to the Americas, and in the Caribbean plantations they produced sugar for consumption in Europe. When slavery was abolished in the British Empire, it was replaced by a system of indentured labour: low-caste 'coolies' from southern India were shipped to east and south Africa and the Caribbean to work on the colonial plantations under conditions not much different from slavery.

In his savage indictment of colonialism, Frantz Fanon claimed that Europe was 'literally the creation of the Third World' in the sense that the 'opulence' of Europe had been fuelled by material wealth and labour from the colonies, 'the sweat and the dead bodies of Negroes, Arabs, Indians and the yellow races.'[1] Not too dissimilar views were held by a man far more moderate and irenic than Fanon-Sir Mohammed Iqbal, the poet-philosopher behind the concept of Pakistan, and a man who, like Fanon, owed much intellectually to the West, and even received a knighthood from the British. In his *Persian Psalms*, published in1927, he declared:

> 'Against Europe I protest,
> And the attraction of the West.
> Woe for Europe and her charm,
> Swift to capture and disarm!
> Europe's hordes with flame and fire
> Desolate the world entire...'[2]

While profits flowed from the colonies to the 'mother' country, there was also a flow of people from the latter to the former. They went as administrators, soldiers, merchants, adventurers, missionaries, scholars, chaplains, and settlers. In some societies European colonialism penetrated more deeply than in others. The forms of colonial domination varied widely, from rule (with varying degrees of harshness) through native elites such as in the Indian subcontinent to the 'gun-boat diplomacy' and 'opium wars' of the 1840s in east Asia and the wholesale massacre of tribes by white settlers in southern and western Africa.

---

1   Franz Fanon, *The Wretched of the Earth*, trans. C. Farrington (New York: Grove Press, 1963) pp.76-81
2   Quoted in Francis Robinson, 'Present Shadows, Past Glory', *The Times Literary Supplement*, September 6 2002, p.15

Repressive alien rule, however, required some concessions and also the partial incorporation of the ideas and practices of the dominated. The Italian Marxist Antonio Gramsci's work on hegemony has inspired much post-colonial analyses of colonial societies and has fuelled resistance movements and postcolonial discourse. Hegemony is power achieved through a combination of coercion and consent. Gramsci noted that subjectivity and ideology are absolutely central to the processes of domination. He argued that the ruling classes achieve domination not by coercion alone, but by inducing subjects to be willing collaborators in their subjugation. Ideology is the medium through which the ideas of the ruling class are transmitted and accepted by the ruled, and is crucial in manufacturing consent. [3]

Modern-day Britons, like their predecessors in the time of the Raj, have an inveterate tendency to think of their empire as essentially benign. Yes, there were unfair trading practices, the occasional military atrocity, and the corrupt administrator or vicious police officer, but these were blemishes on an otherwise disciplined and high-minded enterprise. Once they had abolished the trade in slaves, which had been the mainstay of their colonial economy until it became economically unviable, the British made the abolition of slavery a moral crusade, part of their 'civilizing mission' in Africa and elsewhere.

'Postcolonialism'

Postcolonial studies take their cue from the internal contradictions of colonial discourses, whether those discourses be found in the form of official governmental papers, Victorian novels, traveller's journals, missionary newsletters, scientific catalogues, historical reports or biographical narrative. However the term 'postcolonial' has become fraught with controversy in academic circles. If it is used in a purely temporal sense- meaning the historical process of political decolonisation- then debates rage as to whether 'postcolonial societies' are truly independent, or still locked into forms of economic and political dependence that were established in the heyday of colonialism. If 'postcolonial' is used in a critical sense - meaning the continuing process of resistance to hegemonic discourse - then debates rage as to whether it is adequate to understanding both the past and the present oppressions of 'postcolonial societies'.

---

3   Antonio Gramsci, *Selections from the Prison Notebooks*, edited and translated by Quintin Hoare and Geoffrey Nowell Smith (London: Lawrence & Wishart, 1971)

Many contemporary commentators generalise about colonialism from their knowledge of it in a specific place or time. Thus, in the work of Gayatri Spivak, a prominent 'postcolonial' literary critic, nineteenth-century India, and particularly nineteenth-century Bengal, becomes the model for theorising about the colonised world. Postcoloniality becomes a vague condition of people anywhere and everywhere, and the specificities of locale do not matter.

Although postcolonial studies is such a wide-ranging discipline, encompassing everything from literary analyses to contemporary critiques of global capitalism, some themes prominent in most postcolonial writings are:

(1) Understanding colonialism as an ongoing *subjective* phenomenon. As the Caribbean novelist George Lamming put it, 'the colonial experience is a *live* experience in the *consciousness* of these people... The experience is a continuing *psychic* experience that has to be dealt with and will have to be dealt with long after the actual colonial situation formally "ends".'[4]

In this context, some writers have suggested that we interpret the 'post' in 'postcolonialism' as the contestation of all forms of colonial domination, thus integrating the history of anti-colonial resistance with contemporary resistances to Western imperialism and to dominant Western (especially American) culture. This would allow us to include people geographically displaced by colonialism such as African-Americans or people of Asian or Caribbean origin in Britain as 'postcolonial' subjects although they live within metropolitan cultures. Jorge de Alva suggests that postcoloniality should 'signify not so much subjectivity "after" the colonial experience as a subjectivity of oppositionality to imperializing/colonizing (read: subordinating/subjectivizing) discourses and practices'. He justifies this by arguing that new approaches to history have discredited the idea of a single linear progression, focusing instead on a 'multiplicity of often conflicting and frequently parallel narratives'. Therefore, he suggests that we should 'remove postcoloniality from a dependence on an

---

4   Quoted in P. Hulme, 'The profit of language', in J. White (ed.), *Recasting the World: Writing After Colonialism* (Baltimore, MD and London: John Hopkins University Press, 1993) p.120

antecedent colonial condition' and 'tether' it to post-structuralist theories of history.[5]

So, a strong strand in postcolonial theory shifts the focus from social locations and institutions to individuals and their subjectivities. In part the dependence of postcolonial theory upon literary and cultural criticism, especially post-structuralist approaches, is responsible for this shift.

(2) The reading of colonialism itself as a *literary text*. This follows from the fact that what is circulated as 'postcolonial theory' has largely emerged from within English literary studies departments in American and European academies, and from the 'post-structuralist turn' in many of these departments. Colonialism is analysed as if it were a text, a method of representation of colonial subjects. These representations are available to us through a range of writings, as mentioned above. Even when writings on colonial or postcolonial discourse do not explicitly privilege the textual, they do so implicitly by interpreting colonial relations through literary texts alone. 'The meaning of "discourse" shrinks to "text", and from there to "literary text", and from there to texts written in English because that is the corpus most familiar to the critics... colonialism-as-text can be shrunk to a sphere away from the economic and the historical, thus repeating the conservative and humanist isolation of the literary text from the contexts in which it was produced and circulated.'[6]

(3) The recovery of the 'other' that was suppressed by colonialist discourse. No area of human knowledge was left untouched by colonialism. Much of what was considered scientific, objective knowledge - especially knowledge about other peoples and their societies- was embedded in colonial practices that accompanied, justified and used that knowledge in the service of colonial domination.

The Palestinian-American Edward Said's hugely influential book *Orientalism: Western Conceptions of the Orient*[7] inaugurated a new study of colonialism. Said looked at how representations of the

---

5   J.K. de Alva, 'The postcolonization of the Latin American experience', in G. Prakash (ed.) *After Colonialism: Imperial Histories and Postcolonial Displacements* (Princeton, NJ: Princeton University Press, 1995) p.245

6   Ania Loomba, *Colonialism/Postcolonialism* (London and New York: Routledge, 1998) pp.96,97

7   Harmondsworth, London: Penguin, 1978

'Orient' in European literary texts, travelogues and other writings contributed to the creation of a dichotomy between Europe and its 'others', a dichotomy that was central to the maintenance and extension of European hegemony over other lands.

Said's principal focus was on Napoleon's expedition to Egypt in 1814 and the subsequent transformation of studies on 'Middle Eastern' societies. When Napoleon arrived in Egypt in 1798- on board a ship called *L'Orient*- he brought with him an entire scientific academy, the Institut d'Egypt. By occupying Egypt he planned to damage British trade in the eastern Mediterranean and threaten British India. But he also presented himself to the Egyptian people as their liberator, restoring a state of true civility to the 'Orient'. In the words of the massive *Description de l'Egypte*, which appeared in twenty-three volumes between 1809 and 1828, Egypt, which had 'transformed its knowledge to so many nations', was now, under its Mamluk and Ottoman rulers, 'plunged into barbarism'. From this unhappy condition Napoleon, the 'Muhammad of the West', as Victor Hugo later called him, had come to release it and, while he was there, 'to make the lives of the inhabitants more pleasant and to procure for them all the advantages of a perfect civilization.'[8]

Using Foucault's method of discourse analysis (which traces the way that power works through language, literature, culture and the institutions which regulate our daily lives), Said moved away from a narrow understanding of colonial authority. He showed how it functioned by generating a discourse about the 'Orient'- structures of thinking which were manifest in literary and scientific writings and more specifically, in the creation of Oriental studies. Said's basic thesis is that Orientalism, or the 'study' of the Orient, was an instrument of Western imperialism, in the form of 'an accepted grid for filtering through the Orient into Western consciousness' whereby, in setting out to 'discover' the cultures of Asia, Orientalists reshaped an Orient to suit their own Occidental prejudices.

So, 'knowledge' about non-Europeans was part of the process of maintaining power over them. It was 'a political vision of reality whose structure promoted the difference between the familiar (Europe, the West, "us") and the strange (the Orient, the East, "them")... When

---

8   *Orientalism*, pp.81-5

one uses categories like Oriental and Western as both the starting and the end points of analysis, research, public policy... the result is usually to polarize the distinction- the Oriental becomes more Oriental, the Westerner more Western - and limit the human encounter between different cultures, traditions, and societies.'[9]

Said's assault led to a spectacular volte-face in Departments of Oriental Studies in the 1980s as Western academics suddenly became conscious of their political positions. The term Orientalism today carries heavy pejorative overtones, while the 'Orientalist is judged in much the same terms as those Orientals whom he himself, according to Said, once sought to judge, study, depict, discipline, illustrate, contain and represent.'[10]

Towards a More Nuanced Understanding

Said's work, and the numerous extensions of his work to other fields, is of permanent merit in so far as it highlights the way that representations of the East as the essentialized and stereotypical 'Other' of the West serve to suppress the rich complexity and diversity of both the East and the West. Any writer who claims to have uncovered the 'essence' of, say, 'the Chinese mind' or 'American culture' needs to be treated with a heavy dose of scepticism, even ridicule. Similarly, all binary oppositions (e.g. 'Europe' and 'Asia', 'us' and 'them', 'tradition' and 'modernity') can no longer be regarded as fixed and stable.

However, there are also several ambiguities, tensions and omissions in Said's work. These have been submitted to many rigorous critiques, and I do not intend to rehearse those criticisms here.[11] What I shall do in the remainder of this essay is to make some brief observations on the ironies and paradoxes involved in both Orientalist and anti-Orientalist discourses, especially in relation to Indian religions and politics, and then to dialogue with contemporary academic discussion about 'postcoloniality' as it engages with theology.

---

9   Ibid.pp. 43-6
10   Charles Allen, *The Buddha and the Sahibs* (London: John Murray, 2002) p.4
11   Representative critiques can be found in Michael Sprinker (ed.) *Edward Said: A Critical Reader* (Oxford: Blackwell, 1992); Carol A. Breckenridge and Peter van der Veer (eds.), *Orientalism and the Postcolonial Predicament* (Philadelphia: University of Pennsylvania Press, 1993)

(1) Stress is often laid on how aggressive European powers were in the past in relation to other continents. However, what made possible the growth of British colonialism in the period between the end of the Napoleonic Wars (1812) and the First World War (1914) was the relative absence of conflict between the European powers. Linda Colley notes that 'In every century during the first and second millennium - with only one conspicuous exception- Europeans have devoted more energy to hating, fighting and invading each other, than to hating, fighting and invading peoples outside Europe.'[12] Colley also notes that the lower ranks of British soldiers, mostly Irish working-class men, experienced the brutality of the British Raj (for example, routine corporal punishment) far more than most Indians: 'British soldiers stationed here often perceived themselves as the lowest of the low. They were captives of an alien environment, captives of their own state, and captives of a situation where their sepoy counterparts were in some respects better treated because they were deemed more important.'[13]

(2) Postcolonial writings routinely ignore the native colonial narratives and practices which British colonialism, simultaneously, both displaced and re-awakened. The Orientalist discourse, as depicted by Said and his followers, tends to be a merely Western construction imposed on an Oriental *tabula rasa*. But Orientalist productions were shaped by native elites (religious pundits and rulers) on whom foreign scholars had to depend. The native ideologies which influenced, informed and resisted Orientalist positions (often in order to protect their own hegemonies) are often absent in post colonialist narratives. The goal of the traditional Hindu king was universal empire, and south-east Asia experienced the ravages of Hindu, Muslim and Buddhist empire-builders long before the advent of the Europeans. Well before the 'Anglicists' appeared in India with their notorious project of 'forming a class of persons, Indian in blood and colour, but English in taste, in opinions, in morals, and in intellect'[14] the priestly Brahmanical ideologues were subverting vernacular cultures through the imposition of Sanskrit (the so-called 'language of the gods'). As

---

12   Linda Colley, *Captives: Britain, Empire and the World 1600-1850* (London: Jonathan Cape, 2002; Pimlico edition, 2003) p.310
13   Ibid.p.316
14   Thomas Babington Macauley (1835), 'Minute on Indian Education' in Bill Ashcroft, Gareth Griffiths and Helen Tiffin (eds.), *The Post-Colonial Studies Reader* (London and New York: Routledge, 1995) p.430

one scholar of Indian religions notes: 'Sanskrit was the principal discursive instrument of domination in premodern India and.... it has been continuously reappropriated in modern India by many of the most reactionary and communalist sectors of the population.'[15]

Ironically, 'to ignore the role played by Asians themselves in the construction of Orientalist discourses results not only in the myth of the passive Oriental but also perpetuates precisely the East-West dichotomy that is such a feature of Orientalist discourses.'[16] The construction and the appropriation of Orientalist discourses by different, competing groups (both for colonial and anti-colonial ends) followed convoluted and multiple trajectories. A simplistic association of Orientalist discourses with Western colonial aspirations masks both the massive debt that present academic scholarship and Asian religious communities owe the early Orientalists, but also fails to appreciate the way that discourses develop and are transformed over time.

In his fascinating story of the discovery of 'Buddhism' in India and Ceylon by Western scholars, both humanists and Christian missionaries, Charles Allen poses the question: 'What Professor Said and his many supporters have consistently failed to ask is where we would be *without* the Orientalists,' for it was they who 'initiated the recovery of South Asia's lost past.'[17]

'Thanks to the efforts of men like Jones, Buchanan, Prinsep, Cunningham and Marshall, as well as of those who have followed them, the great Buddhist monuments of Ajanta, Sanchi and Sarnath are now visited and admired by hundreds of thousands of visitors each year. Many Indian nationals seem unimpressed-perhaps India has so much antiquity that they have become blasé, or perhaps they have yet to understand the richness of their heritage. But the pilgrimage trails that Fa Hian and Huan Tsang trod so long ago are now followed by thousands of new pilgrims, some of them tourists but many more of them Buddhists, drawn from all over the world.'[18]

---

15 Sheldon Pollock, quoted in David Smith, *Hinduism and Modernity* (Oxford: Blackwell, 2003) p.92
16 Richard King, *Orientalism and Religion: Postcolonial Theory, India and 'the mystic East'* (London and New York: Routledge, 1999), p.158
17 *The Buddha and the Sahibs* , op.cit., pp.4-5
18 Ibid.p.292

(3) Orientalist scholarship led to the creation of 'Hinduism' as a 'world religion' and its identification with a corpus of Sanskrit texts (Vedas, Upanishads, etc) painstakingly edited and translated into Western and modern Indian languages. These texts were now bestowed with canonical authority over 'Hindu' practices in a manner similar to the Semitic faiths. It led to the periodization of Indian history into Hindu, Muslim and British stages, with 'Indian civilization' identified with the earliest stage and the Muslim and Christian presence effectively occluded. In the hands of men like Swami Vivekananda (1863-1902), founder of the Ramakrishna Mission, and Mohandas Gandhi, Orientalist notions of India as 'otherworldly' and 'spiritual', in contrast to the 'nihilism' and 'materialism' of modern Western society, were embraced and presented as India's gift to humankind. Thus colonial stereotypes were perpetuated and re-employed in the anti-colonial nationalist struggle.

Moreover, it was an Orientalist history that attributed the modern concept of 'tolerance' to Hinduism even though as a doctrinal notion it had no specific place in Hindu discursive traditions. Modern Hindu thinkers have come to interpret hierarchical relativism in Hindu discourse in Orientalist terms, as 'tolerance'. Wilhelm Halbfass argues convincingly that the step to reconcile all religious and philosophical traditions was not taken prior to the colonial period.[19] And the characteristic manner in which it was done was by relativising truth-claims and including all religious traditions within the Vedanta, the spiritual 'essence' of 'pure' philosophical Hinduism, as in Radhakrishnan's famous saying: 'The Vedanta is not a religion, but religion itself in its most universal and deepest significance.'[20]

A comparable role was played by Zen Buddhism in the period of Meiji nationalism in Japan. Aspects of Buddhism attractive to Western audiences - 'mystical' experience and the absence of institutional religious forms - have been marketed in Europe and the United states by prolific authors such as D. T. Suzuki. Vivekananda's neo-Vedanta and Suzuki's version of Zen became the stereotypical 'religions of Asia' for spiritually jaded Westerners seeking an exotic alternative to institutional Christianity. 'Suzuki's abstract, universalized and non-institutionalised "Zen", like the neo-Vedanta of Vivekananda and

---

19 W. Halbfass, *India and Europe* (Albany, New York: SUNY Press, 1988) pp. 403-418
20 Quoted in Ibid..409

Radhakrishnan, provided a classic example of the universality of "mysticism", increasingly conceived as the experiential "common core" of the various "world religions".' [21]

(4) Anti-colonial narratives, such as secular or religious nationalisms, are embedded in specific histories, and cannot be collapsed into some pure oppositional essence. Nationalist struggles in Algeria against the French were very different from Indian resistance to the British, and neither can be equated to Korean and Chinese struggles against Japanese imperialism. (Indeed non-Western forms of imperialism are glaring in their omission from postcolonial studies). Slavery in Africa was begun by Arabs, and continued by Arabs after its abolition in the British empire, often with the connivance of local tribal leaders. The attempts by Christian missionaries such as Buxton and Livingstone to spread commerce along with Christianity as a means of breaking the economic stranglehold of slavery has usually been vilified by postcolonial writers who have not paid attention to the specific context in which these missions worked.

(5) Many postcolonialist writers display a marked indebtedness to the early work of Michel Foucault. Foucault conceived of power in modern societies, not as emanating from a centralized authority, but as dispersed by a kind of capillary action throughout the spheres in which it operates. '[T]he manifold relationships of force that take shape and come into play in the machinery of production... are the basis for wide-ranging effects of cleavage that run through the social body as a whole.' [22]

In the field of colonial discourse analysis, Homi Bhabha has developed Foucault's ideas to argue (against Said) that colonial power and discourse were not so all-encompassing that the colonized were left without any resources for resistance. Bhabha applies the Derridean notion of "*differance*', denoting the endless differentiation and deferral of meaning within texts in order to highlight the inherent ambivalence of colonial discourse. Since discourses cannot be controlled once they have entered the public arena, they can be contested, appropriated and even inverted by others. There is always a gap in the blanket of power through which the repressed can return. Bhabha suggests that colonial authority is rendered 'hybrid' and "ambivalent' by the process of

21 King, *op.cit.*, p.156
22 Michel Foucault, *History of Sexuality*, Vol.1 (Harmondsworth: Penguin, 1978) p.94

replication of colonial identities, thus opening up spaces for the colonised to subvert the master-discourse.[23]

Thus for Bhabha the key to anti-colonial resistance is the subversive *mimicry* of the colonialist by the colonized native. Hybridity 'reveals the ambivalence at the source of traditional discourses of authority and enables a form of subversion, founded on that uncertainty, that turns the discursive conditions of dominance into the grounds of intervention.'[24] The ambivalent figure of the English-speaking Indian in British India represents the instability of the colonizer-colonized dichotomy, and it is not surprising that it is he or she (and not the vernacular-speaking subalterns) who are central to Bhabha's analysis of colonial discourse. Bhabha and other English-speaking writers of the Indian diaspora can now invest themselves with new heroic identities as subversive voices for the voiceless, even in their own mimesis of Western academic aridity.

Since, in Bhabha's view, it is the *failure* of colonial authority to reproduce itself completely that allows for subversion, he has been criticized for not considering alternative sources of anti-colonial intellectual and political activity. More seriously, his conception of the agency and resistance of the colonized as primarily mimesis seems to require the continuing authority of the colonial discourse, thereby (paradoxically) reinscribing colonialism as a totalizing process. The totalizing discourse cannot be contested from any other position. As Benita Perry puts it, the only option available to the colonized subject is 'to place incendiary devices within the dominant structures of representation and not to confront these with another knowledge.'[25]

(6) It is ironic that while many postcolonial writings, especially those influenced by post-structuralist readings of texts and histories, stress fragmentation, diversity and 'hybridity', they routinely posit a

---

23 Homi Bhabha, 'Signs taken for wonders: questions of ambivalence and authority under a tree in Delhi, May 1817', in *Critical Inquiry* 12.1, 1985, pp.144-165, abridged version in Ashcroft et al. (eds), *The Post-Colonial Studies Reader*. Homi Bhabha, 'The other question: difference, discrimination and the discourse of colonialism', in Francis Barker (ed.), *Literature, Politics and Theory* (London: Methuen, 1986). Reprinted in Padmini Mongia (ed.) *Contemporary Postcolonial Theory: A Reader* (London: Hodder Headline Press, 1996)

24 'Signs taken for wonders', p.36

25 Benita Perry, 'Problems in current theories of colonial discourse', in *Oxford Literary Review* 9, 1987, p.43; abridged version in Ashcroft et al. (eds) *The Post-colonial Studies Reader*, p.43

universal 'postcolonial subject', a 'postcolonial condition', even a 'postcolonial woman'. Writing about the 'universalizing tendency' in Bhabha's work (and other writings inspired by it), Ania Loomba makes the pertinent observation that this 'derives partly from the fact that in it colonial identities and colonial power relations are theorised entirely in semiotic or psychoanalytic terms. While theories of language and the psyche have given us sophisticated vocabularies of subjectivity, we also need to think about how subjectivities are shaped by questions of class, gender and context. We need to peg the psychic splits engendered by colonial rule to specific histories and locations. In making the point that "there is no knowledge - political or otherwise - outside representation" Bhabha reduces colonial relations to a linguistic interchange.'[26]

Postcolonialism is, therefore, a word that is useful only if used with qualifications. If the word is uprooted from specific historic and cultural locations, the nature of 'postcolonial' oppressions cannot be properly investigated, and the term may well obscure the very relations of domination that it seeks to uncover. Postcoloniality, like patriarchy or racism, is articulated alongside other economic, social, cultural and historical factors, and therefore, in practice, it works differently in different parts of the world.

(7) Bhabha, Spivak and many others who are known as 'postcolonial theorists' are affluent, self-exiled Asians ensconced in the Western academy. Indeed, Arif Dirlik asks: 'When exactly does the "postcolonial" begin? ... I will supply here an answer that is only partially facetious: when Third World intellectuals have arrived in First World academe.'[27] It is tempting to suggest that much of their popularity in Western academic circles (much more so than in the 'Third World') is due not only to their playing on 'postcolonial Western guilt' but also on the romantic image of the intellectual 'exile', epitomizing the fissured identities and hybridities generated by colonial dislocations and celebrated in some postmodern works. 'But while of course there are themes in common across different kinds of diasporic experience and exiles, there are also enormous differences between them. The experiences and traumas generated by the single

---

26 *Colonialism/Postcolonialism*, op.cit. p.179
27 Arif Dirlik, 'The postcolonial aura: third world criticism in the age of global capitalism', *Critical Inquiry*, 20, ii, Winter 1994.

largest population shift in history- the division of India and Pakistan-are quite different from that of immigrants from once-colonised nations to Europe and America.'[28]

Dirlik argues that the 'language of postcolonialism is the language of First World post-structuralism'. The 'cult of the fragment' tends to confuse ideological metanarratives with the actualities of power. Moreover, the purely theoretical rejection of global narratives can end up silently supporting the latter. Therefore, postcolonialism, which appears to critique the universal pretensions of Western knowledge systems, and 'starts off with a repudiation of the universalistic pretensions of Marxist language ends up not with its dispersal into local vernaculars but with a return to another First World language with universalist epistemological pretensions.'[29]

(8) Nationalist movements, and the postcolonial nation-state, have duplicated the exclusions of European colonialism. It could be argued that the continuing exclusions and oppressions of caste and patriarchy in India far outweigh, for ordinary folk, the oppressions of colonial rule. Women's movements, peasant struggles or caste- and class-based dissent, both during and after colonial rule expose the distance between the rhetoric and the reality of the nation-state. In recent years, the effort to uncover the histories and standpoint of people excluded by nationalist projects has multiplied across the disciplines. 'Subalternist histories' have attempted to tell other stories of rebellion and struggle, as well as to relate them to the narratives of nationalism and decolonisation. The Subaltern Studies Collective, a group of (largely diaspora) Indian historians, is perhaps the best-known example of this approach. It shifts the crucial divide from that between colonial and anti-colonial to that between 'elite' and 'subaltern'.[30]

However, several attempts to write such 'histories from below' have come close to essentialising the identities of peasant or tribal communities. On the other hand, postmodernist and post-structuralist moves to dissolve all unities into more complex heterogeneities, and to

---

28 Loomba, op.cit., p.180
29 Dirlik, op.cit.p.342
30 Ranajit Guha, one of the founders of the project, inaugurated the widespread use of the term 'subaltern' in postcolonial studies, which he defined as 'the demographic difference between the total Indian population and all those we have defined as elite'. Cf. Ranajit Guha, 'On Some Aspects of the Historiography of Colonial India', in R. Guha (ed.), *Subaltern Studies*, Volume 1 (New Delhi: Oxford University Press, 1982, p.8

speak of the self as merely 'the dispersed effect of power relations', have been seen by some as undermining the agency of the oppressed. The problem of aligning oneself with a radically anti-representationalist stance is aptly summed up by the feminist scholar Nancy Hartsock: 'Why is it that just at the moment when so many of us who have been silenced begin to demand the right to name ourselves, to act as subjects rather than objects of history, that just then the concept of subjecthood becomes problematic?'[31]

Postcolonial theory thus seems to be riven by a clash of agendas: between, on the one hand, a romanticized search for a heroic underclass and, on the other, a radically deconstructionist stance that remains sceptical of the existence of anything outside of discursive power relations. And here we come back full circle to Said himself. For Said vacillated between an acknowledgement that 'the Orient' is more than a colonial cognitive construction (i.e. there *are* authentic features to be discovered) and a Foucauldian, anti-representational position. But, as several critics have noted, his passionate moral outrage reveals a cosmopolitan humanist in the Enlightenment tradition. In an interview in 1986, he remarked: '*Orientalism* is theoretically inconsistent, and I designed it that way; I didn't want Foucault's method, or anybody's method, to override what I was trying to put forward. The notion of a non-coercive knowledge, which I come to at the end of the book, was deliberately anti-Foucault.' [32]

Ten Theological Reflections

We have seen that 'postcolonial criticism' has come to mean different things to different people, depending on the context. For some, it is fundamentally a challenge to Eurocentric ways of thinking, speaking and acting; to others, resistance to the totalizing discourses of the nationalist project or to the epistemic violence of Western imperialism; to still others, a generalised commitment to an emancipatory, egalitarian political agenda.

(1) Whatever its use or abuse, postcolonial criticism reminds us as Christian theologians that our social location shapes our speech. Hence it is important to pay attention not only to *what* is said in

---

31 Nancy Hartsock, 'Foucault on power: a theory for women?' in Linda J. Nicholson (ed.), *Feminism/Postmodernism* (London: Routledge, 1990) p.163
32 Interview with Said in Imre Salusinzsky, *Criticism in Society* (London: Methuen, 1987, p.137), cited in King, op.cit. p.84

theological discourse but also *who* says it and *how* that discourse may be received/perceived by others. For example, who is the 'we' in statements such as 'we believe that...' or 'we have moved beyond outmoded notions like...'? All theology has to be self-reflexive, in the Gadamarian sense of recognizing our prejudices rather than aspiring to a God-like 'objectivity'.

In a work criticizing those who seemed to write unaware of the way in which their view of the past was influenced by their understanding of the present, the eminent British historian Herbert Butterfield (himself a Christian) made the interesting observation that 'it is not a sin in a historian to introduce a personal bias that can be recognised and discounted. The sin of historical composition is the organization of the story in such a way that bias cannot be recognised.'[33]

(2) The 'we' in Christian speech always arises out of local contexts, but it is disciplined by our belonging to the global body of Christ. The Church is the only truly global community, and it is largely a church *of* the poor. Far more spectacular than the resurgence of Islam- or the spread of New Age spiritualities in the Western world and Hindu or Buddhist nationalisms in the Indian subcontinent - has been the growth of indigenous Christian movements in the postcolonial South.

Recent mission historians have drawn attention to this southwards shift of the centre of gravity of the Christian Church. It was in the decades following decolonisation that Christianity outpaced Islam in Africa. As I.M. Lewis once noted, the 'total effect of the *pax colonica*, as much involuntary as intended, was to promote an unprecedented expansion of Islam', and that 'in half a century of European colonization Islam progressed more widely and more profoundly than in ten centuries of precolonial history.'[34] The astonishing expansion of African Christianity is a vivid rebuttal of the Darwinian thesis about the survival of the fittest. The main bearers of African Christianity seem to have been the young, women, the oppressed and others lacking monetary and organizational power. This is in striking contrast with the spread of Islam in Africa or Hindutva among the Indian middle-class diaspora.

---

33   H. Butterfield, *The Whig Interpretation of History*, quoted in David Brown, *Tradition and Imagination: Revelation and Change* (Oxford University Press, 1999) p.22
34   I. M. Lewis, *Islam in Tropical Africa*, London, 1966, cited in John Mbiti, *African Religions and Philosophy*, Nairobi, 1989, p. 256

These facts seem to be hidden from postcolonial theorists as well as the media. In typically Orientalist fashion, Christianity is naively identified with Europe and the United States in most postcolonialist writings, and all Christian missionaries of the colonial age are assumed to have been mere pawns in the hands of colonial administrators. No major work of Indian history, whether nationalist or subaltern, even mentions the contribution of, say, Ziegenbalg and Plütschau, Carey and the Serampore mission, Schwartz, Beschi, Pope, Caldwell and a host of other foreign Christians who pioneered education for women and dalits, opposed both the Orientalists and the Anglicists in rescuing vernacular tongues and cultures from relative oblivion.

There are of course many shameful stories to be told of Western missionary complicity in colonial practices of domination. But the many stories also of missionaries and local Christian leaders in India, Africa or the South Pacific who courageously defended native interests and combated racist theories and stereotypes propagated by their fellow-countrymen are missing from the anti-Orientalist corpus.[35] As for Africa, 'It is remarkable,' observes Andrew Walls, 'that the immense Christian presence in Africa is so little a feature of modern African studies, and how much of the scholarly attention devoted to it is concentrated on manifestations that in Western terms seem most exotic.'[36]

(3) The Gospel narrative embodies a vision of human dignity, equality and flourishing that is fundamentally anti-hierarchical and destructive of all forms of paternalism and domination. The belief in human equality is not self-evident, nor is it derived from empirical observation or introspection, but stems from fundamental theological convictions, in particular that God ascribes infinite worth to human beings and loves them equally as a father with his family. The great biblical truths of Creation, Incarnation and Resurrection have empowered human beings in the face of suffering and oppression. 'When an indigenous Christian leader from northern Argentina was once asked what the

---

35 For these accounts see, for example, the essays by Jane Samson and Brian Stanley in Brian Stanley (ed.) *Christian Missions and the Enlightenment* (Grand Rapids, Mi and Cambridge, UK: Eerdmans, 2001)

36 Andrew F. Walls, 'Structural Problems in Mission Studies' in *The Missionary Movement in Christian History: Studies in the Transmission of Faith* (Edinburgh: T & T Clark and New York: Orbis, 1996) p.150

Gospel had done for his people, he replied that it had enabled them to look the white person fully in the eye.'[37]

'The ideal of equality,' notes the social theologian Duncan Forrester, 'haunts any culture that has been shaped or influenced by Christianity.'[38] Of course there is much in the Bible that is seemingly contradictory, and has lent itself in Western history to the buttressing of hierarchical attitudes and oppressive hierarchical structures. However, the dominant narrative stream in the biblical traditions encourages a strongly egalitarian *direction* of thought, which functions especially to critique relationships of privilege. The tendency of biblical thought, Richard Bauckham argues, 'is not in support of but away from hierarchical structures in human society, and biblical images of God's rule function not to legitimate human hierarchy, but to relativize and delegitimize it.'[39]

Thus, even when the Bible depicts God in images of hierarchical, masculine power and authority- Lord, King, Father - the way the language is used is subversive of all human hierarchies. To call God King is to say that all human beings are equally God's subjects. To call God Father is to say that all human beings are equally God's children. The egalitarian thrust to New Testament teaching is grounded, first of all, in Jesus' proclamation and enactment of God's Reign which draws into the new community of a renewed Israel all who are estranged from God and one another, forgotten and excluded by human sin. It finds its culmination in the conviction that 'while we were yet sinners, Christ died for us' (Rom 5:8), so that one's fellow human being must now be valued as one for whom Christ died.

Bauckham has shown that this opposition to hierarchy assumes two different forms in both the Old and New Testaments. The first is a radical rejection and delegitimation of hierarchical structures altogether and calls for egalitarian structures and relationships instead. The second is a pragmatic and provisional acceptance of such hierarchies but in order to transform them *from within* towards the

---

37 J. Andrew Kirk, *What is Mission?: Theological Explorations* (London: Darton, Longman and Todd, 1999) p.71
38 Duncan B. Forrester, *On Human Worth: A Christian Vindication of Equality* (London: SCM Press, 2001) p.109
39 Richard Bauckham, 'Egalitarianism and Hierarchy in the Bible', in *God and the Crisis of Freedom: Biblical and Contemporary Perspectives* (Louisville: Westminster John Knox Press, 2002) p.118

ultimate goal of equality. These different strategies are united in sharing a common goal.

The greatest tragedy in the following centuries of the Christian era in the West was that the power of prevalent custom in Greco-Roman societies prevented the Church from following through on what its own teaching taught it to do. This was especially true when the Church became a powerful institution. Far from undermining from within the prevailing social order, the Church conformed to that order, allowing the dominant religious culture to define relationships within the Church. Theologies produced from within national churches have tended to buttress the status quo and silence opposition from below.

(4) This equality of respect extends to languages and cultures. The West-African scholars Lamin Sanneh and Kwame Bedako have shown how revolutionary is the Christian attitude to religious language. That ordinary people (including the 'subalterns' of postcolonial discourse) should *understand* the word of God in their own speech was a view with momentous consequences for social and cultural awakening. God's universal purposes did not supplant their own social enterprises but included them. 'It is one of the great historical truths of our day that otherwise obscure tribes, without a claim to cosmopolitan attainment, should find in indigenous particularity the sole grounds for appeal to international recognition.'[40]

Elsewhere, Sanneh notes: 'The fact of Christianity being a translated, and translating, religion places God at the centre of the universe of cultures, implying free coequality among cultures and a necessary relativizing of languages vis-á-vis the truth of God. No culture is so advanced and so superior that it can claim exclusive access or advantage to the truth of God, and none so marginal or inferior that it can be excluded. All have merit; none is indispensable. The vernacular was thereby given the kiss of life.'[41]

(5) The Christian understanding of sin and evil enables us to give a more nuanced perspective on the politics of domination and exploitation. The subaltern/elite binary opposition is itself destabilized, as not only is the subaltern situated along many

---

40 Lamin Sanneh, *Encountering the West* (London: Marshall Pickering, 1993) p.119
41 Lamin Sanneh, *Whose Religion is Christianity?: The Gospel Beyond the West* (Grand Rapids: Eerdmans, 2003) pp.105-6

conflicting axes of domination (gender, class, ethnic, etc) but one can be a subaltern in one context and an elite in another. The subaltern is best regarded as a shifting signifier, not a homogeneous community devoid of its own hierarchies and hegemonies. 'The very condition of being oppressed,' writes the political scientist Fred Halliday in a critique of some types of anti-Orientalism, 'in a collectivity as much as in an individual, is likely to produce its own distorted forms of perception: mythical history, hatred and chauvinism towards others, conspiracy theories of all stripes, unreal phantasms of emancipation .... Those forces that are often deployed against the oppressive and global- the local, the indigenous, the communal - may therefore conceal as much confusion, and as much instrumentalism and coercion, as the structures they claim to challenge.'[42]

This is why political ideologies that either take a Manichean approach to the oppressed and the oppressor, or emphasize the structural aspects of evil at the expense of the personal, are not radical enough. Yesterday's poor migrant in Europe, for instance, is often today's most rabid opponent of new asylum-seekers. To use the old Exodus paradigm, it is easier to get the people out of Egypt than Egypt out of the people. Of course one must be committed to *both*, and the precise strategies adopted would vary from context to context. If conservative Christians needed to be challenged to see how the 'individual' cannot be conceptualized without the structural, those influenced by a secular liberal agenda that can only see people as 'victims' of evil systems (or as 'sinned against' and never as 'sinners' except in the sense of passivity in the face of structural evil), need to be challenged to recover a biblical realism about our own responsible agency as well as our endless capacities for self-deception and self-destruction. This is not, of course, to say that our sins are equal, or that we all sin in the same way. Rather it is to point to the complex ambivalences of human beings. It is interesting that Nancy Hartsock argues that Foucault's rather pessimistic world is one 'in which things move, rather than people, a world in which subjects become obliterated or, rather, recreated as passive objects, a world in which passivity or refusal represent the only possible choices.'[43]

---

42 Fred Halliday, *Islam and the Myth of Confrontation: Religion and Politics in the Middle East* (London: I. B. Tauris, 1996) p.5
43 Nancy Hartsock, 'Foucault on power: a theory for women?' in Linda J. Nicholson (ed.), *Feminism/Postmodernism* (London: Routledge, 1990) p.167

Postcolonial historians often want to have their cake and eat it. It is commonly argued that the peasant, the tribesman, the woman, or the working-class man is an 'autonomous' agent of resistance. Yet, when it comes to sentiments like patriotism, nationalism or pan-national religious identities, of which they disapprove, that agency is denied to ordinary people who are treated as docile victims of state or elitist manipulation. In fact, while wars started by states have certainly reinforced such sentiments, 'patriotism, jingoism, and inter-communal hatreds have also proceeded from the people and influenced otherwise cautious statesmen, rather than vice versa …. Nationalism was not simply a sentiment forced on hapless and naive peoples by wicked power-brokers and greedy capitalists.'[44]

It was the recognition of the universality of sin, variously expressed in different cultures, that prevented more Biblically-minded Christian leaders from joining the racist chorus of British imperialism in the nineteenth-century. David Smith writes: 'It is worth recalling that when the founder of the Salvation Army, William Booth, published his controversial study of social conditions in British cities and gave it the title *In Darkest England and the Way Out*, he was deliberately challenging racist models of humankind and subverting Stanley's depiction of the African continent. The darkness, Booth suggested, is not limited to distant lands which we classify as "uncivilized"; it is found in the back alleys of the slums of London and, indeed, when the causes of the degradation of the poor are investigated, we shall have to conclude that it is also to be found in Whitehall and the City of London.'[45]

(6) We have observed that postcolonial criticism is often impaled on the horns of the following dilemma: whether to align itself with humanist notions of an autonomous, sovereign subject and so run the risk of subsuming heterogeneous identities and histories into an abstract 'essentialism', or of embracing a post-structuralist anti-humanism and so denying any universal moral platform from which to contest the material and epistemic violence of the colonial encounter. Gayatri Spivak has argued for a 'strategic essentialism' as a way of

---

44 C.A. Bayly, *The Birth of the Modern World, 1780-1914* (Oxford: Blackwells, 2004) pp.280-1
45 David W. Smith, 'Fundamentalism and the Christian Mission', *Against the Stream: Christianity and Mission in an Age of Globalization* (Leicester, UK: Inter-Varsity Press, 2003) p.105-6

resolving this dilemma: that while postcolonial theory favours the decentred, free-floating 'postmodern self', emancipatory practice requires us to adopt an essentialist stance. We saw that Said distanced himself from Foucault precisely because of his commitment to a universal human solidarity.

It is important to note that this dichotomy between humanist and anti-humanist, which generates a corresponding split between theory and practice for the postcolonial critic, is itself a result of marginalizing other discourses from the secular Western academy. Christian theology points in a direction beyond this dichotomy. What it means to be human can only be grasped in its full scope on the basis of the gracious work God, Father, Son, and Spirit, in God's saving self-communication with us. For the Triune God, plurality is not a foreign territory. When the early theologians used the word 'person'- whether persons in God or human beings - they meant a 'distinct identity', an otherness, which only made sense *in relationship*. But 'person' soon became a word for an otherness that was an aloneness, a naked individuality of the mind closed in on itself. Trinitarian theology insists that a 'person' is *not* an autonomous centre of consciousness; rather, persons are necessarily woven into the lives of other persons. They participate in one another's lives, whether they realize it or not. In the eternal life of self-giving and self-responsive love that we call 'God', the Three so 'indwell' one another that we cannot really speak of any One of them without implying something about the other Two as well.

Thus, although human persons are not to be confused with the divine persons, there is a distinctively Christian ontology of humanness that points beyond both humanism and anti-humanism. There is no autonomous, sovereign human subject at the centre of history, nor is there an abstract 'human nature' that lies behind the variety of human histories. Not only does all human life and history take place within the divine economy, which is definitive of what it is to be and act humanly, but our human solidarity is constituted *relationally*, both in relationship to God and to one another.

(7) Who speaks for the 'voiceless'? That is a topic that has provoked heated argument among postcolonialist theorists and subaltern historians. Given the roots of postcolonial theory in literary and cultural criticism, it is not surprising that Gayatri Spivak argues not

140

only for the impossibility of recovering premodern histories and identities untainted by the imperial encounter, but that precisely because the subaltern cannot speak, it is the duty of postcolonial intellectuals to represent her/him. This invites charges of paternalism and a self-serving academic anti-Orientalism. Indeed, some critics have suggested that the new discipline of 'postcolonial literature' is less a subversive field than a career move for largely upper-class Asians in American universities.[46] Commenting on the way Derridean and Foucauldian texts are appropriated, Russell Jacoby observes, somewhat cynically:

'In a world composed of texts, no texts are central. Conversely, if there is no centre, anything is marginal to something. This is music to the ears of many academics, who, no matter how esteemed and established, often claim to be marginalized, victims lacking proper recognition and respect. They see themselves as outsiders, blasting the establishment. Like uptown executives cruising around in pricey jeeps and corporate lawyers in luxurious utility trucks, they pose as rugged souls from the back country; they threaten the seats of power as they glide into their own reserved parking spots.'[47]

In the postcolonial lexicon, 'diasporic hermeneutics' and the experience of 'hybridity' and 'hyphenated identities' by Third World academics and artists living in the West seem to have a privileged place. However, it is salutary to remember that it is Africa, not Europe or North America, that is host to the largest number of refugees in the world (with millions of Christians among them), followed by South Asia. These are people whose experiences are remote from those of cosmopolitan postcolonial theorists, the majority of whom have fled not persecution or war but less lucrative academic jobs in their native countries. The absence of the former from postcolonial discourse betrays the parochialism, indeed Eurocentrism, of much postcolonial writings.

(8) Similarly, who speaks for 'Third World theology'? A number of dictionaries and anthologies that have appeared in recent years on 'Third World theology', 'Asian theology', and the like, are usually written by Western Christians or by non-Western Christians domiciled

---

46 Cf. Russell Jacoby, *The End of Utopia: Politics and Culture in an Age of Apathy* (New York: Basic Books, 1999) p.123
47 *Ibid.* pp.121-2

in Western academies. There is also a curious selectivity shown in the way these anthologies are usually compiled. 'Asian theologies' are taken to be theologies addressing what is called, in typical Orientalist fashion, the 'Asian context'; and the latter is typically reduced to poverty, women's empowerment, environmental justice and the presence of ancient 'world religions' ('Hinduism', 'Buddhism', 'Islam' to some extent). Western theologians feel free to write on such 'Asian issues', but Asian theologians who address other issues, local or global, tend to be marginalized in such anthologies. Moreover, only if one were to espouse the typical Western secular liberal agenda (e.g. same-sex partnerships, abortion 'rights', the equal validity of all religious worldviews) can one acquire the status of being a 'progressive' theologian. Hence the huge gulf between those who profess to speak for the 'Third World' Church (in most ecumenical theological conferences) and the 'Third World' Church itself.

Undoubtedly, postcolonial criticism helps us to appreciate the hybridized and fluid nature of identity-formation in many societies today under the impact of globalization and the flow of peoples. The division of societies into fixed 'people-groups' (very common in a number of imported missiologies) is sociologically flawed, and the idea that mission should have as its goal the 'planting of churches' within such 'people-groups' is theologically deeply problematic.

But this is also where some African and Asian attempts at Christological reconstruction in the name of 'contextualisation' suffer from a credibility problem. Their theological method begins with an African or Asian 'reality' that is assumed to be given and unchanging, and then searches for a Christology that would be 'relevant' or 'meaningful' to that context. Cecie Kolie writes of fellow African theologians: 'Since their communities cannot name Christ personally without going to the Bible and the catechisms, they do just the opposite, and attribute to Christ the traditional titles of initiator, chief, great ancestor, and so on, that they would *like* to see him given in their communities. Once more we impose on our fellow Africans the way of seeing that we have learned from our Western masters.'[48]

Kenneth Ross points out that this runs counter to the approach adopted by the Nicene theologians. The latter did not see their task as

---

48   Cecie Kolie, 'Jesus the Healer', in Robert J. Schreiter ed., *Faces of Jesus in Africa* (London: SCM, 1992) pp.141-2

primarily one of creative construction but of articulating, faithfully and coherently, a reality that was *already there*, expressed in the life and worship of the believing community. Ross suggests that this offers a 'liberating methodology' for African (and, I would add, other) theologians: 'They are not required, on the one hand, to present a pre-packaged Christ who remains wrapped up in terminology and conceptuality that has been constructed elsewhere. Nor are they required, on the other hand, to work out their own Christology on the basis of their own assessment of what will be relevant to the African situation. Their task is, in fact, to bring to the clearest possible expression a reality which is already powerfully evident within African life, namely God's revelation in Jesus Christ.' [49]

Ross' own field studies in northern Malawi showed how Christians there showed a marked preference for biblical titles such as Saviour, Lord, Healer, even Messiah, over against those which most African theologians have advanced as truly 'African' Christologies: ancestor, chief, and so on. Such data could be interpreted as evidence of the intellectual passivity of the Christians, or it could be interpreted, as Ross himself does, 'in terms of a community being drawn to biblical vocabulary and conceptuality as a means of accurately stating what it has to say about the reality of Jesus Christ'.[50] Ross points out that a comparable development in patristic theology would be the way in which the initial cultural inclination to understand Jesus in terms of the 'Word' (*Logos*) gradually gave way to the Old Testament idiom of 'Son' as this could better articulate the relational understanding of God which was found in the Gospel.

'So in African Christology it may well be that the categories which at first seem to make sense of Jesus in African terms gradually give way to the more biblical categories which are preferred .... As the Bible comes to occupy an increasingly formative place in the life of the community, its vocabulary and conceptuality may come to displace or revise the terms and categories which initially were predominant. It may be that we are entering a time when biblical vocabulary and concepts are *no less* indigenous than those derived from the African tradition!' [51]

---

49 Kenneth Ross, *Here Comes Your King!: Christ, Church and Nation in Malawi* (Blantyre, Malawi: Christian Literature Association, 1998) p.31
50 Ibid.p.24
51 Ibid. p.25

Thus, as Jesus Christ enters as a participant into the vernacular world of a community, becomes known there, and steadily comes to occupy a central place in the spiritual and moral universe of the people, his identity and significance comes to be recognized. In authentic contextualisation, not only is there a conceiving of Jesus Christ in terms of 'traditional culture', there is also a re-conception and re-orientation of that culture in terms of the apostolic tradition.

(9) Postcolonial criticism has brought its deconstructive scrutiny to bear on the Bible.[52] Here the typical approach boils down to: (a) Reading the Bible as just another text on par with other literary and 'religious' texts, carrying no special status or authority in the life of the Church; (b) Showing up the contradictions in the biblical text, and especially the places where the voices of the oppressed are silenced; (c) Rewriting the text, or jettisoning whole texts altogether, in the service of a 'domination-free' political agenda. Here the postcolonial critic simply mirrors the violence of colonial hermeneutics. He/she positions him/herself above the text as its judge, extracts what is useful for his/her political purposes, and, paradoxically, wields the secularist liberal worldview of the academy (itself part of the colonial legacy) to outlaw all other theological voices. So, while difference is celebrated in theory, in practice differences tend be trivialized and subsumed under an old-style global humanism. There is nothing in the text, or any 'Other' beyond the text, that can anymore disturb and challenge the postcolonial reader's life-world.

Moreover, there is surely a huge difference that the *aims* of biblical study make to the interpretation of the biblical text. Postcolonial criticism may be justified in approaching the Bible as a general text and not as the canonical, self-authorizing text of the Church. Nevertheless, there is a world of difference in the power-dynamics involved between, say, reading the Bible in order to hear God speaking to me and to discover what obedience to God means for me today, and reading it as a university lecturer in a religious studies department who is driven by the academic pressure to both defend the relevance of my subject and also be 'original' and prolific in my publications so as to obtain tenure. It is strange that, for all its obsession with issues of

---

52 Cf. Fernando F. Segovia (ed.), *Interpreting Beyond Borders : The Bible and Postcolonialism 3* (Sheffield: Sheffield Academic Press, 2000); R.S. Sugirtharajah, *Postcolonial Criticism and Biblical Interpretation* (Oxford: Oxford University Press, 2002)

power/knowledge, postcolonial biblical criticism has not applied its post-structural 'hermeneutics of suspicion' to its own academic context.

(10) There is a great need to develop local theologies and missionary practices that receive from all that is best in other cultures and contexts, while being relevant to one's own. In the Church we now have a 'hermeneutical community' that is global in scope and character, so we can test the local expressions of Christian faith against one another, thus manifesting the true catholicity of the body of Christ. The way we become truly global Christians is by seriously engaging with our *local* contexts as members of a *global* community that has re-defined our identities and interests.

This implies, on the one hand, that no local theology (whether German, Brazilian, or Korean) can ever become normative universally even though it may have universal relevance. On the other hand, since all *Christian* theologies endeavour to speak truthfully (albeit, in broken speech) of the universal God whose Triune nature is disclosed, redemptive purposes effected, and divine authority mediated, through a historically-grounded narrative, the theologian - as a member of the Christian worshipping community - indwells that narrative herself and seeks to articulate it, in dialogue with other voices, past and present. Since scripture invites us to see ourselves as living in the final (eschatological) act of the divine drama of redemption, we are at liberty, within that final act, to create new scenes as we experience new contexts. However, the credibility of such new scenes depends on, firstly, how faithful in character they are to the overall story-line and, secondly, how richly they further our obedience to the original vision of how the play will end. What we are *not* at liberty to do is to act as if the play starts with us. To change the story-line, import scenes from other plays, or re-write the ending, is to act in another play altogether.

Musical improvisation, too, provides an apt analogy for scripture reading and the theological task, and this is well expressed by the New Testament scholar, Bishop Tom Wright:

'As all musicians know, improvisation does not at all mean a free-for-all where "anything goes", but precisely a disciplined and careful listening to all the other voices around us, and a constant attention to the themes, rhythms and harmonies of the complete performance so far, the performance which we are now called to continue. At the same time, of course, it invites us,

145

while being fully obedient to the music so far, and fully attentive to the voices around us, to explore fresh expressions, provided they will eventually lead to that ultimate resolution which appears in the New Testament as the goal, the full and complete new creation which was gloriously anticipated in Jesus' resurrection... All Christians, all churches, are free to improvise their own variations designed to take the music forwards. No Christian, no church, is free to play out of tune.'[53]

Finally, let us return to Frantz Fanon. In the conclusion to his *The Wretched of the Earth*, Fanon thundered, 'Let us decide not to imitate Europe; let us combine our muscles and our brains in a new direction... Let us not pay tribute to Europe by creating States, institutions, and societies which draw their inspiration from her.'[54] Ironically, wherever the anti-colonial project has tried to isolate itself completely from European ideas and institutions (as in Cambodia or Burma, to take two examples from recent Asian history), the results have been tragic for its own people. Fanon's Afrocentricity was a mirror-image of the worst forms of colonial Eurocentricity. But 'Europe' is not a simple thing, any more than is 'Africa'; in the last century it has spawned both universalism and relativism, cosmopolitanism and chauvinist nationalism, tolerance and genocide. There is the Europe of massive cruelty, and also the Europe 'with the capacity to step outside its exclusivity, to question itself, to see itself through the eyes of others.'[55] Cultural essentialism is a myth, but it is a myth that dies hard. Which Europe prevails, under current globalizing conditions, will have profound consequences for which Africa (and which Asia and which Latin America) emerge in the twenty-first century.[56]

53 N.T. Wright, *Scripture and the Authority of God* (London: SPCK, 2005) p.93
54 Fanon, op.cit., pp.313,315
55 L. Kolakowski, *Modernity on Endless Trial* (Chicago: University of Chicago Press, 1990) p.18
56 This paragraph is an adaptation from an earlier essay. Cf. Vinoth Ramachandra, 'Learning from modern European secularism: a view from the Third World church" in *European Journal of Theology*, VII:2, 2003

NEW ZEALAND

REFLECTIONS FROM 'FAR AWAY' ISLANDS

Kathy Ross

Introduction

As I write this paper, sitting in my home in Auckland, Aotearoa/NZ I anticipate leaving to go and live and work in a far away island, across many seas. It is the conviction that this is our calling from God that is drawing us to come and work with CMS (B); to leave our homeland of Aotearoa to venture across the world and settle in a strange land. More than two hundred years ago, on Christmas Day 1814, it was in the other direction that the first CMS missionaries landed on other far away islands to preach the gospel to the native Maori people of Aotearoa. Comings and goings, crossing borders and boundaries, translations and transmissions have seen the gospel flourish in many far away lands so that now the centre and the periphery, the core and the margins are no longer clearly defined. What is 'near' and what is 'far away' can no longer be defined by Euro-American criteria as we live in a world with shifting centres and margins for a world Christian. Not only are the centres and margins shifting but world Christianity must be interpreted by a plurality of models. World Christianity is becoming increasingly diverse and long gone are the days where we can understand and interpret Christianity only within a Western framework. Lamin Sanneh observed that "people want to interpret Christianity by standards of exegesis and doctrine familiar to them, something that the Christendom model of the church warranted."[1] However, the West can no longer impose its own definitions and structures on peoples and cultures far removed from its centres and standards. The global reality today is far more complex.

Sanneh argues that "global Christianity" and "Christendom" are interchangeable.[2] While Jenkins asserts that global Christianity

---

1 L Sanneh, *Whose Religion is Christianity? The Gospel Beyond the West,* (Grand Rapids:Eerdmans, 2003), 35.
2 Ibid,, 23.

represents the next Christendom to be found predominantly in the South, Sanneh argues, on the other hand, that global Christianity is "the faithful replication of Christian forms and patterns developed in Europe."[3] He prefers the term "world Christianity" which he defines as "the movement of Christianity as it takes form and shape in societies that previously were not Christian, societies that had no bureaucratic tradition with which to domesticate the gospel ... World Christianity is not one thing, but a variety of indigenous responses through more or less effective local idioms, but in any case without necessarily the European Enlightenment frame."[4] Todd Johnson and Sandra Kim, in a recent article in the *International Bulletin of Missionary Research,* argue that either term, global Christianity or world Christianity, can be used interchangeably and with positive connotations. They claim that "we truly live in the age of global Christianity, of world Christianity, or worldwide Christianity, of Christianity on six continents...What this great fact means to particular Christians will continue to challenge both local and global expressions of the faith."[5] Global Christianity or world Christianity? Old Christendom or next Christendom? Maybe the terminology confuses rather than clarifies at times. I would like to present four vignettes, all experienced in an Australasian context, which show, I believe, that the boundaries are still fuzzy, that old and new Christendoms overlap, that the new may be transforming the old in unexpected ways. As Sanneh has commented, "the diverse, complex reality of the world Christian resurgence defies any simple explanation, or, indeed, any single cultural formulation."[6]

A Garden Party

My recent attendance at a garden party at the Anglican Bishop of Auckland's residence caused me to reflect long and hard on the local and global expression of the faith in the Anglican Church today. The particular occasion was the book launch of a book on Mrs Eliza Cowie, wife of Bishop Cowie, Bishop of Auckland from 1870-1902. Lady Beverley Reeves, the author, herself a former Bishop's wife, wanted to tell the story of this remarkable woman and restore her to our history.

---

3   Ibid, 22
4   Ibid., 22
5   T Johnson and S Kim, "Describing the Worldwide Christian Phenomenon", *International Bulletin of Missionary Research,,* Vol 29, no 2, April 2005, 84.
6   L Sanneh and J Carpenter (eds), "The Current Transformation of Christianity" in *The Changing Face of Christianity, Africa, the West and the World,* (Oxford:OUP, 2005), 213.

Despite the derision of my children at attending a garden party in the Bishop's gardens which, to them, reeked of colonialism, caste and the old Christendom perhaps, I was pleased to attend because of my keen interest in women's history – and it was an interesting occasion. Apart from the author's grandchildren and the Auckland Girls' Choir (quaintly dressed in period costume for the affair) I was probably the youngest there in an all white audience. The nature of the event caused me to stop and think about the generally declining and ageing congregations of our Anglican church in Aotearoa/NZ. It also made me think of our own particular local history and how the Anglican church of Aotearoa, New Zealand and Polynesia is working out its own identity in this particular context.

Christmas Day, 1814, the Rev Samuel Marsden held the first service at Oihi, in the Bay of Islands where he preached and was translated by the Maori chief Ruatara, who had invited him to come. Straight away the gospel was being shaped by two cultures, the preacher and that of the translator. Two years later, Marsden noted

> On Sunday morning, when I was upon deck, I saw the English flag flying, which was a pleasing sight in New Zealand. I considered it as the signal and dawn of civilization, liberty and religion, in that dark and benighted land. I never viewed the British Colours with more gratification; and flattered myself they would never be removed, till the Natives of that island enjoyed all the happiness of British subjects.[7]

This reflection by Marsden immediately shows the ambiguous relationship between Christianity and colonisation. As Davidson commented, "The beginning of the work of the missionaries is inextricably connected with national identity and the possibility of future incorporation of Maori as 'British subjects. Maori will then enter the 'Happiness' enjoyed by 'British Christians.'"[8] Indeed the first CMS missionaries promoted civilisation as the means of evangelism but this all changed in 1823 with the arrival of the Rev Henry Williams and others who focussed primarily on evangelism, Bible translation and literacy. The growth of the mission church was rapid so that by the 1850s, according to Allan Tippett, 70% of Maori were Christian.

---

7 Samuel Marsden, *Missionary Register,* (November, 1816), 470-1.
8 Allan K Davidson, "Christianity and National Identity: The Role of the Churches in 'the Construction of Nationhood.'" in , J Stenhouse, B Knowles and A Wood (eds), *The Future of Christianity,* (Adelaide:ATF Press, 2004) 16.

The mission church grew partly through using the Maori language in liturgy and preaching, partly through the distribution of Maori Bibles and partly through what New Zealand historian Michael King described as "the high degree of spiritual energy which Maori had always shown, and their deep interest in religious questions and practice."[9] However, British settlers were arriving in New Zealand in droves, eager for land and a new way of life, far from the constrictions of British society.

In 1840 the Treaty of Waitangi was signed between Maori and the Crown in an honest attempt to pre-empt land, social, economic and judicial problems that could arise from the pressure of a rapidly increasing settler population. The Treaty was translated by the CMS missionary, the Rev Henry Williams rapidly and overnight. There are some significant differences between the two versions. The part played by Williams has been much debated. He later claimed that he showed Maori "the advantage to them of being taken under the fostering care of the British Government, by which act they would become one people with the English, in the suppression of wars, and of every lawless act; under one Sovereign, and one Law, human and divine."[10] The purposes of the Treaty were:

> To provide foreigners with rights to live in the land and to specify the conditions; to assist in determining the authority of the Crown within the land; to provide law and order for all; and to clarify the rights and to protect the interests of Maori as the 'people of the land', including fisheries, forests, lands and other *taonga* (treasures).[11]

The Treaty is still a very significant document in the history and contemporary life of Aotearoa/NZ in both society and the Anglican Church. Although the CMS missionaries encouraged the development of a native church, the pressure of *Pakeha* (white) immigration and the arrival of Bishop Selwyn, as a settler Bishop, with his policies of blending, meant that the Maori church radically declined and was expected to be assimilated into the settler church. Meanwhile this

9   Michael King, *The Penguin History of New Zealand,* (Auckland:Penguin, 2003), 144.
10 Hugh Carleton, *The Life of Henry Williams,* (Auckland:Wilsons and Hortons, 1887), 2:14.
11 T John Wright, "Historical Consciousness and Patterns of Engagement: Lessons learnt in the Anglican Church in Aotearoa New Zealand and Polynesia" in *Journal of African Christian Thought,* Vol 7, No 1 June 2004, 47.

settler church was struggling to adapt to this far away land. The Christianity that was brought to Aotearoa/NZ was generally an Anglo-Celtic, Eurocentric import – called by two NZ historians, a "transplanted Christianity."[12] By the 1970s this Eurocentric import, this relic of Christendom was failing. Increasing immigration from the Pacific Islands, and later from South East Asia as well as a renaissance of Maoridom was forcing Aotearoa/NZ to reconsider its own identity both as a nation and within the Anglican Church.

During the latter part of the nineteenth and most of the twentieth century Maori lost their voice in the Anglican Church.[13] In 1857, the first Constitution of the Anglican Church did not have one Maori signature. In 1928, one Maori Bishop, a suffragan Bishop, was appointed and he could only minister within the dioceses at the invitation of the respective *Pakeha* Bishops. It was not until 1964 that this Bishop had his own seat in General Synod and in 1978 the Bishopric of Aotearoa, *Te Pihopatanga o Aotearoa* was established. In 1984, the Bicultural Commission of the Anglican Church on the Treaty of Waitangi was set up to look at the constitution of the church. The Council of *Te Pihopatanga o Aotearoa,* in its submission made the following poignant statement:

> The Council asks the Commission to set out clearly for the Church an understanding of the concepts of *tangata whenua* [people of the land] and *manuhiri* [guests], so as to overcome the problems associated with the treatment of Maori as *manuhiri,* or honoured guests, in a Church which was Maori in the beginning in Aotearoa.[14]

And so in 1992 the Anglican church in Aotearoa, New Zealand and Polynesia took a radical step and revised its constitution to comprise three equal *Tikanga* (groupings, strands) – Maori, Pakeha and Pasifika. "It was the culmination of 180 years of interaction between Maori and Pakeha, of promises made and broken, of hopes unfulfilled, and of an interaction between Church and state which had been ill defined and little understood."[15] The Constitution drew on principles from the

---

12 A K Davidson and P J Lineham, *Transplanted Christianity: Documents illustrating Aspects of New Zealand Church History,* (Auckland:College Communications, 1987)
13 By the end of the 20th century, Maori form 15% of New Zealand's population of 4.1 million.
14 "Historical Consciousness", 50
15 Ibid, "Unpublished Statement", 50.

Treaty of Waitangi, especially those of partnership and bicultural development. The new Constitution is an attempt by the Anglican Church to address past injustices, to provide for equity and to enable power-sharing. Each tikanga has its own congregations, its own structures, training facilities and models – they are, in effect, self-governing, self-propagating, self-supporting and self-theologising.[16]

There is much debate about our three tikanga church. Some laud it as a paradigm of equity, justice and reconciliation. Others claim it is a form of *apartheid*. Others ask about the inclusion of our many other ethnic groups now residing in Aotearoa/NZ. Bishop Muru Walters, a current Maori bishop wrote that the Constitution "recognises the need to redeem the Church's unjust treatment of Maori over many years. This redemptive theological model enables the Church to say sorry, seek forgiveness and reconciliation for its historical injustice to Maori."[17] Is this new structure of the Anglican Church truly a prophetic voice to the nation (and the world?), a voice from the margins that is engaged and engaging with social injustices and siding with the poor? The Anglican *Hikoi* of Hope in 1998 was a high profile, public event which included the three *tikanga*. This was a march which took in the length and breadth of our country, and which incorporated many ordinary New Zealanders as we marched to Parliament to protest about social injustices, high unemployment, spiralling crime and loss of hope in many communities. Was this a prophetic act by the Anglican Church? I would like to say yes. And in part it was. However, I will never forget marching on the *hikoi,* and being shouted at in fury by some passing cyclists, "What about the cathedral?" The Anglican cathedral in Auckland was spending $8 million on a building project at the same time as the *hikoi*! This irony was evident to many. Somehow, we have not shaken off the Christendom model, the old relationships and maybe even irrelevant priorities. Are we still suffering from Sanneh's global Christianity - the faithful replication of Christian forms and patterns developed in Europe? Are we operating from within the old Christendom or the

---

16 See, for example, Ilaitia Sevati Tuwere, *Vanua:Towards a Fijian Theology of Place,* (Institute of Pacific Studies, Suva:University of the South Pacific, 2002) Ree Bodde (ed) *Thinking Outside the Square: Church in Middle Earth,* (Auckland: St Columba's Press and Journeyings, 2003), Janet Crawford (ed) *Church and State: te tino rangatiratanga,* (Auckland:College of St John the Evangelist, 1998)

17 "Historical Consciousness", Muru Walters, 'New School of Theology: A Te Waka Matauranga (Tikanga Maori Ministry Board) Response', (unpublished, July 17, 2002), 56.

new Christendom with an attempt at indigenous structures? Will these new structures lead to new life?

Well, I hope so. The new three Tikanga structure is only 13 years old and maybe this structure will offer new ways forward in the future. However, despite its acknowledgement of the ambiguous relationship with colonialism, its separation from any formal relationship with the state and its deliberate move to recreate its structures, the Anglican Church is still in a state of decline and struggling to come to terms with this new era of world Christianity. As far as I can see, our church leaders still look to Euro-America for their models, their sabbaticals, their learning. Few indeed are those who look to those parts of the Anglican Communion that are growing – the next Christendom transforming the old. We seem trapped by a declining Christendom model, still aligning ourselves with Western bishops over such issues as homosexuality without the strength of will to look elsewhere or engage in other debates. Of course, there are large and growing Anglican churches. They are often evangelical, usually have youth pastors and youth programmes and sometimes, strangely, have little interest in social engagement and wider world issues. It is a complex picture and I think I will avoid any more garden parties for a while.

Forty Days of Purpose

I returned from the garden party on Saturday to attend our local Anglican church on Sunday which was embarking on the North American programme, "Forty Days of Purpose." This is based on the book *The Purpose Driven Life* by Rick Warren, founding pastor of Saddleback Church, California, "one of America's largest and best-known churches", according to the description on the back of the book. "*The Purpose Driven Life* is a blueprint for Christian living in the 21st century – a lifestyle based on God's eternal purposes, not cultural values. Using over 1,200 scriptural quotes and references, it challenges the conventional definitions of worship, fellowship, discipleship, ministry and evangelism."[18] The book has sold over a million copies in twenty different languages and has twice received the Book of the Year award from the Evangelical Christian Publishers Association. There are video presentations by Rick Warren, a chapter to read each day for forty days, small group discussion material and

---

18 Rick Warren, *The Purpose Driven Life, What on Earth am I here For?*, (Grand Rapids:Zondervan, 2002), back cover.

even a sermon, kindly prepared by Rick Warren, to be preached by the minister for six Sundays. This programme has been widely used throughout Aotearoa/NZ in churches of many denominations.

Global Christianity or world Christianity? I have no doubt that this is not only a globalised but a globalising form of Christianity. It is a complete North American package, prepacked for immediate consumption. Even its title shows a complete captivity to the North American worldview. Somehow it is hard to imagine a purpose-driven Ghanaian or Nepali Christian. Along with the study material, there is the opportunity to purchase key rings with memory verses, pens and other sorts of "Jesus-marketing" paraphernalia. It offers a completely de-contextualized approach – the stories, the ethos, the simplistic content, the method is all North American – a top-down approach by a North American, Southern Baptist male telling us of God's eternal purposes.

And yet, and yet, I have heard many stories of people's lives being changed and their faith being deepened through using this course, in Aotearoa/NZ. Somehow, despite the crass marketing techniques, and the unashamed North American-ness of its approach, its apparent lack of cross-cultural awareness, God in God's grace has used this approach to deepen people's faith. It puzzles me, it confuses me and it humbles me. Of course, God can use and redeem anything. But perhaps this is an old Christendom programme, suitable for old Christendom churches and I wonder how widely it is used in the Majority world churches.[19]

The Destiny Phenomenon – the Breakthrough Generation
Another interesting phenomenon in the Aotearoa/NZ context is the recent and rapid emergence of the Destiny churches. They first emerged about seven years ago in a provincial city and now there are twenty throughout Aotearoa/NZ and one in Brisbane. They are fast-growing, vocal and visible. They are fairly typical of Pentecostal churches in some ways – they have the devoted pastoral couple as leaders, tithing is emphasized, a kind of prosperity doctrine in terms of generational transfer of wealth is preached, a conservative and legalistic morality is required. The church in Auckland is huge – a converted warehouse seating 1400. Attending a service there is quite an experience – car park attendants and ushers with suits and ear

---

19 The only other translation I could find on the website was into Spanish.

pieces, six huge PowerPoint screens, loud music in hip-hop style, vouchers for free coffee and muffin for visitors (does one normally have to pay?), a large and polished choir performing for the TV cameras (Destiny has its own TV show) and a 60-90 minute sermon accompanied by background music. There are three collections – tithes, offerings and a gold coin donation for the TV show. The theology is triumphalistic assuring them that they are the chosen generation and with many victorious sayings (not Bible verses) painted on the walls around the church, the most revealing and disturbing being, "Eventually everything will come under our influence." The theology could possibly be considered contextual with many assurances that land will be given back to the next generation – although how this will happen is not made clear.

Destiny is unique in that it appeals to mainly Maori and Pacific Islanders. Most of their pastors are Maori. They have a unique blend of conservative religion and an interest in politics. One commentator writes, "Destiny like other Maori Christians see the Treaty as a religious covenant; they defend the Maori right to the foreshore, and are angry at the abolition of appeal to the Privy Council. They believe that by 2050 Maori will be dominant in this country."[20] They also have a political party. This political dimension is not a new thing for Maori religion. Maori prophets in the past have usually addressed political and social dimensions of life.

The church's website is impressive. They have a host of youth and children's programmes, and a good range of social services including budgeting services, housing, a bilingual school, programmes for those just released from prison, Maori song and dance groups, a gym, health and nutrition services. Is this part of the corporate image or is this genuinely holistic? The political website is equally impressive with a range of policies from the right to the left on the political spectrum and on most current issues including the family, justice, welfare, and more contextually peoples of the Pacific, Treaty of Waitangi, nuclear weapons, the environment and GE. The party is unashamedly Christian with strict moral values, an anti-abortion policy, a focus on protecting the family – unusually for Pacific Island and Maori cultures, defined as the nuclear family – a desire to pursue economic excellence

---

20 Peter Lineham, "Wanna be in my Gang? A New Style of Pentecostalism is emerging in New Zealand", *New Zealand Listener,* vol 195, no 3357, 11-17 Sep, 2004, 23-24.

in an open market economy, and a commitment to honour the Treaty of Waitangi as a covenant that is "perpetually relevant and binding."[21]

Is Destiny old Christendom or new Christendom? Is this a truly indigenous response or is it replicating old forms and patterns from Europe? Certainly, aspects of its approach seem to mimic parts of North American Christianity – the beautifully manicured pastors, the mega-church buildings, the triumphalistic theology, the clever use of media. The founder and overall leader of the Destiny churches is now a self-proclaimed Bishop. Is this not buying into the old patterns from Europe? All this power may not be a good thing, but Maori culture has traditionally had strong leaders with ascribed and chiefly status.

For those who come from the margins, from broken or violent homes, from backgrounds of alcoholic and drug abuse, Destiny, with its moralistic teaching and emphatically conservative stance on many social issues, offers a future and a hope. There are many at Destiny who come from these backgrounds and whose lives have been changed. As Jenkins says,

> The most significant point is that in terms of both theology and moral teaching, Southern Christianity is more conservative then the Northern version... The denominations that are triumphing across the global South – radical Protestant sects, either evangelical or Pentecostal, and Roman Catholicism of an orthodox kind – are stalwartly traditional or even reactionary by the standards of the economically advanced nations.[22]

He also wryly comments in his book, that "Western experts rarely find the ideological tone of the new churches much to their taste."[23] This is certainly the case in Aotearoa/NZ where the 'more established' churches look with horror at the statements and behaviour of Destiny such as their "Enough is enough" march on Parliament to protest about the Civil Union Bill which recently became legislation.

As Southern Christianity grows, it will determine its own agenda, structures and patterns. Is this the case with Destiny? Is this a genuine independent church or has it been captured by a neo-colonialism which mimics a North American agenda? The jury is out, and may be for a

---

21 http://www.destinynz.co.nz, accessed 20.4.05
22 P Jenkins, "The Next Christianity" in *The Atlantic Monthly*, October 2002, 59.
23 P Jenkins, *The Next Christendom, The Coming of Global Christianity*, (Oxford: OUP, 2002), 7.

long time. I can only reiterate Sanneh's observation that "the diverse, complex reality of the world Christian resurgence defies any simple explanation, or, indeed, any single cultural formulation."[24]

The Spirituality Revolution[25]

An Australian Roman Catholic nun, connected with our daughter's Roman Catholic school in Auckland, drew my attention to David Tacey's intriguing analysis of contemporary spirituality in the Australian context. The cover of the book is interesting - pure, crystal clear water gushing through a woman's hands. For a pietistic Christian, this could be the cover for a devotional book on deepening your prayer life – evoked by streams of living water. And yet the book is not a Christian book. Tacey is Associate Professor and Reader in Arts at La Trobe University in Melbourne.

He describes himself as "a mystical Christian"[26,] to the dis-appointment of the evangelical students and to the suspicion of the secular students who, he says, "are happy for me to be religious and spiritual at the same time, so long as I do not seek to impose my views on them or to cramp their style."[27]

He offers an insightful critique into the demise of religion in the Western world and argues that the growing interest in spirituality is the sign of a new trend in the West. Perhaps there are signs that some sort of spiritual renewal is emerging in the West – not in the old ways, replicating old paradigms but in fresh and new ways as younger people, especially seek a personal relationship with the sacred. He claims that religion has been rejected as patriarchal, otherworldly, dualist, dogmatic, imposing a metanarrative without giving due recognition to our individual stories, captivated by the spirit of the age.

Religion is hierarchical and elitist. It rules from above...
Religion belongs to a former era in which spiritual authority was invested in authority figures, priests, bishops, clergy, and people freely gave authority to such figures. Now we want to own such authority for ourselves, and for two reasons: the inner authority

24 L Sanneh and J Carpenter (eds), "The Current Transformation", 213.
25 D Tacey, *The Spirituality Revolution - the emergence of contemporary spirituality,* (Australia:HarperCollins, 2003)
26 Ibid., 100.
27 Ibid., 101.

of conscience and spirit is compelling, and people no longer trust old authority figures.[28]

Religion belongs to the old Christendom, especially in the West, now people are thirsting for a new thing. Young people, despite giving up on the institutions of faith, which they see as in need of spiritual renewal themselves, yearn for a renewed and holistic spirituality. He has discovered that "there is a tremendous lack of fit between youth spirituality and religion"[29] and he relates how he teaches a course on spirituality which attracts hundreds of students at his University. He has deliberately named it a course on spirituality to attract a broad and diverse range of students. Religion is not understood very well, but a course on spirituality creates a different dynamic. He claims we are at the stage in the West, where the language of religion can polarize while a study of spirituality allows exploration of points of similarity and difference in a more open environment. He encourages a spiritual awakening that can lead to an interest in religion, "based on personal experience, tolerant towards difference, compassionate towards those who make different choices, and relatively free of ideological fanaticism."[30] This is quite a different approach from Destiny – pursued of course in a different context, among University students.

He begins "inside out ...with the ground of experience."[31] For me, this approach resonates with Stephen Bevans' reflections on the place of the Holy Spirit in our lives and in our world. Bevans argues for the chronological and experiential priority of the Spirit in our lives; that the first way that God reaches out to us in love is through the presence of the Holy Spirit. "The Spirit is divine mystery sent from 'inside' to be mystery fully present and active 'outside' – in the world, in human history, in human experience: the Spirit is God Inside Out."[32] The Holy Spirit will lead us to Christ, to be transformed by Christ and to bear witness to Christ. The Holy Spirit is the life-force of all creation, profound and elemental energy, enabling us to participate in the

---

28 Ibid., 36-7.
29 Ibid., 75
30 Ibid., 77.
31 Ibid., 76.
32 S Bevans, "God Inside Out: Toward a Missionary Theology of the Holy Spirit", *International Bulletin of Missionary Research,* vol 22, No 3, July 1998, 102.

ongoing work of creation. The Holy Spirit enables us to be the people we were created to be. Bishop John Taylor, in his marvellous book on the Holy Spirit, wrote,

> From within the depths of its being [the Spirit] urges every creature again and again to take one more tiny step in the direction of higher consciousness and personhood; again and again he creates for every creature the occasion of spontaneity and the necessity of choice, and at every turn he opposes self-interest with a contrary principle of sacrifice, of existence for the other.[33]

I think this is the kind of spirituality those young people are seeking. Tacey's understanding of a spiritual experience is one that means "a deeper and more profound experience of our ordinary lives."[34] A spirituality that find sacredness in the ordinary, a spirituality as self-sacrifice – "Not 'follow your bliss' but 'thy will be done' is the credo for authentic spirituality"[35] Moreover, it is an engaged spirituality concerned with the welfare of the world, ecological issues, domestic violence, racism, civil unrest. This spirituality compels people to social action, "Private spirituality is revealed as an illusion, or as a transitional stage between a former state of sleep and a future mission of social responsibility and commitment."[36]

This is the kind of spirituality that young people could find in the church, but do not according to Tacey. Like an Old Testament prophet he ventures the following insight

> God might be saying, 'I don't want blind belief, or worshippers who are content with a mere rumour of my existence. I want people to experience me in their hearts and lives; I want transformation, conversion and encounter.' The spirit of God wants to lead us on, and yet our attachment to old forms may be preventing this spirit from being realised.[37]

Again, the "faithful replication of old patterns" are not serving us well in the West. The church is increasingly out of touch, in denial and

---

33 J V Taylor, *The Go- Between God, The Holy Spirit and the Christian Mission*, (London:SCM, 1972), 36.
34 *The Spirituality Revolution*, 78.
35 Ibid., 146.
36 Ibid., 148.
37 Ibid., 192.

unable to respond to the new situation. It may be more fitting for the church to face the crisis and to mourn the passing of the old.

David Hay and Kate Hunt's research on British spirituality is apposite here,

> The people we have been talking to in recent months tell us again and again that the church is out of touch. This may be a wearisome platitude, but perhaps we should face up to the reality behind it. Perhaps the cliché is telling us that we are not in touch with the ways in which God the Holy Spirit is already communicating with his secularised children.[38]

The emergence of models such as ancient/future church and the so-called emerging churches are a recognition that the old patterns are not serving us well.[39] "Futurechurch nz, a platform for emerging churches of spiritual community" has 47 groups listed on its website, along with numerous resources, an e-magazine, blogs and links to over 50 other sites – both national and international.[40] When interviewed on his reaction to the appointment of Cardinal Joseph Ratzinger as the next Pope, Bishop Pat Dunn, Roman Catholic Bishop of Auckland, said it was an "inspired choice." He explained, on national radio, that St Benedict was the patron saint of Western Europe and that by adopting the name of Benedict, the new Pope was foreshadowing his intention to speak clearly to the dying churches of Western Europe.[41]

The old patterns are not serving us well. We are living among the rubble of a bygone era with the remnants of old Christendom soldiering on. Tacey's book gives hints of a new era and a renewed growth in spirituality. The challenge will be for the churches in the West, still generally operating out of the old Christendom paradigm, to recognise this and to make room for its expression – even as some flock to the more established churches to seek refuge in old certainties in a world of uncertainty and disorder.

---

38 Ibid., D Hay and K Hunt, "Is Britain's soul waking up?" *The Tablet,* London, 24 June, 2000, 846.

39 See for example in the Australian and New Zealand context, Frost, M and Hirsch, A *the Shaping of Things to Come, Innovation and Mission for the 21ˢᵗ Century Church,* (Australia:Strand, 2003), Taylor, S *The Out of Bounds Church, Learning to Create a Community of Faith in a Culture of Change,* (Grand Rapids:Zondervan, 2005)

40 http://www.futurechurch.org.nz, accessed 21.4.05

41 Bishop Pat Dunn, "Morning Report", Radio NZ, 20.4.05.

Conclusion

There is a lot going on out there! Even in our South Pacific context, there is a wide range of approaches and a clash of Christendoms as old paradigms and new struggle to find their place in the South Pacific sun. What is clear is that there are many alternative ways of being a Christian. Many are disillusioned with old assurances, while some are seeking just that. Others are looking for community, identity and hope. The four phenomena I have considered, while all operating contemporaneously, straddle the old and new christendoms. Is there room for both?

World Christianity is emphatically neither monocultural nor monolithic, and 'the next Christendom', however we may understand that word, is already upon us.[42] It is variegated, colourful; a many-splendoured thing. At times it defies definition and analysis. Perhaps I am a naïve optimist, born and brought up in the new world, far from the former (?) centres of power and influence, although shaped by them nonetheless, but I feel cautiously hopeful for the future of world Christianity. The growth of the churches in the South, the ability of the Anglican church in Aotearoa/NZ to take an honest look at itself and remodel its structures, the flourishing of the independent churches and the increased interest in spirituality by young people, all point to a promising future. In humility we have to acknowledge that, "the diverse, complex reality of the world Christian resurgence defies any simple explanation, or, indeed, any single cultural formulation."[43] And our challenge, as missiologists and as world citizens, is to faithfully practise our vocation of world Christianity.

---

42 See Johnson and Kim, "Describing the Worldwide Christian Phenomenon", 81 for a
     fuller discussion.
43 L Sanneh and J Carpenter (eds), "The Current Transformation", 213.

LATIN AMERICA

MISSION FROM THE PERIPHERY: THE THEOLOGY OF ORLANDO COSTAS AND INFEMIT

Allen Yeh

Philip Jenkins's book, *The Next Christendom*, is an important contribution to our knowledge of the movement of Christianity to the non-Western world, and as such it provides a suitable theme for this conference. However, Jenkins was, in my personal awareness of this topic, only the most recent exponent of this theme. Earlier, I can recall Dana Robert, Lamin Sanneh, and Andrew Walls,[1] among others, all striking this same chord. Only it took Jenkins's book to bring this fact to light among the secular media, so the book is significant for the effect it has produced.

Yet in terms of chronology, there were missiologists some twenty years earlier than Jenkins who already recognized this global trend in Christianity. One such person was Orlando Costas, a Puerto Rican missiologist who died in 1987. Costas is significant not only because of his ministry and writings, but because he was non-white and non-Western, at a time when not many minorities were wielding such a strong influence.[2] He died of cancer at age 45, but during his short lifetime, he wrote ten books and hundreds of articles. He pastored five different churches, both in Latin America and in the U.S.; he was a professor at three different seminaries; and he earned four academic

---

1 See, for example, Dana Robert's article "Shifting Southward: Global Christianity Since 1945" in the *International Bulletin for Missionary Research*, April 2000; Lamin Sanneh, *Translating the Message* (Orbis, 1998), and the more recent *Whose Religion is Christianity?* (Eerdmans, 2003); Andrew Walls, *The Missionary Movement in Christian History* (Orbis, 2000) and its sequel *The Cross-Cultural Process in Christian History* (Orbis, 2002).

2 I use the word "minority" loosely because white people have, for some time now, been ethnic minorities in this world. But in the U.S., the word "minority" has come to denote a non-white person, at least for now; a new term will have to be coined once the sum total of the blacks, Hispanics, Asians, and Native Americans outnumber the whites. Already, whites are a minority in some major cities, like Los Angeles, or in some states, like Hawaii.

degrees, including a doctorate in theology. He was dually ordained in the American Baptist and United Church of Christ denominations. The last seminary that he taught at, Andover Newton Theological School, elected him to be academic Dean, and thus he became the first non-white Dean of any mainline theological school in the U.S.

I am currently writing my doctoral thesis at Oxford University on Orlando Costas, and I chose Costas precisely because I wanted a missiologist who truly spoke from the perspective of the Third World. When I was in seminary, my former missions professor[3] urged me, when I was researching a suitable topic, to choose a missionary who actually came *from* the non-Western world, rather than a Western missionary who tries to adapt him or herself to the non-Western world. And my professor's words have been proven wise as Costas has embodied, in the 1970s and 80s, what Jenkins would write about some 20-30 years later. This study is both ontological and epistemological, and thus will encompass two parts: Costas's life and his thinking.

The Life of Orlando Costas: Four Conversions

To properly understand Orlando Costas's theology, it is necessary to have an idea of the circumstances of his life and the influences surrounding him. Costas himself described "four conversions" in his life: conversion to Christ; conversion to culture; conversion to the world; and conversion to Macedonia. The story of his life can be built around these four conversions.

Orlando Costas was born on the "enchanted island" of Puerto Rico on the 15th of June, 1942, as the oldest of five children. Life was not easy economically, and his family was, like so many other Puerto Ricans, compelled to move to the mainland of the United States to make a better living. They settled in the New York City / Tri-State area which is home to a large population of Puerto Ricans today.[4] While his family was not irreligious, Costas himself had no firm committed Christian faith until he attended Billy Graham's New York crusade on 8 June 1957 in Madison Square Garden.[5] There, Costas

---

3   Dr. Timothy Tennent at Gordon-Conwell Theological Seminary in South Hamilton, Massachusetts.
4   Adalberto López, *The Puerto Ricans* (Cambridge, MA: Schenkman Publishing Company, Inc., 1980), p. 158: By 1970, there were more Puerto Ricans in New York City than in the Puerto Rican capital city of San Juan.
5   This was Billy Graham's longest-ever Crusade, lasting nightly for 16 weeks.

had the first of his "four conversions": conversion to Christ.[6] Billy Graham issued a call for audience members to dedicate their lives to the Lord, and Costas responded. Two years later, he felt a call to the ministry and eventually became an ordained minister.

Orlando Costas did not stop with one conversion, however. Although born in Puerto Rico, he spent his formative teenage years in the U.S. and attended schools like Bob Jones and Nyack. He decided to return to Puerto Rico to finish his undergraduate education at the Inter-American University, and that is where he experienced his second conversion: conversion to culture. He realized that he was not an Anglo-American; that he straddled a divide and really had two cultures. The U.S. passport that he carried belied the fact that his roots were Latin. He was bilingual in English and Spanish, and in fact would later publish his books in both languages, but the Spanish ones came first. His conversion to culture was important because it helped him "kindle a passionate love for the lands south of the Rio Bravo."[7] He rediscovered his roots and became truly bicultural.

The third conversion was his conversion to the world. Orlando Costas became the pastor of a Hispanic church, the *Iglesia Evangélica Bautista* in the south side of Milwaukee, Wisconsin. He "set out to change Milwaukee's Spanish speaking community from one without a voice in city politics to a cohesive group with representatives on many of Milwaukee's antipoverty groups."[8] He was soon elected to the community's Social Development Commission as the first-ever representative for poor Latinos in Milwaukee.[9] Frustrated with the lack of cohesion among the Latin community, he also organized a Latin American Union for Civil Rights in emulation of the African-American model.[10] This led him "to discover the world of the poor and the disenfranchised as a fundamental reference of the Gospel. [He] came to realize that the Christian mission had not only personal, spiritual, and cultural dimensions, but also social, economic, and

6   Dannette Costas, "Missiology: From the Underside of History" [interview with Dr. Orlando E. Costas], (Newton Centre, MA: 29 November 1985), p. 1
7   Orlando Costas, "Conversion as a Complex Experience—A Personal Case Study" in John R.W. Stott and Robert Coote, eds., *Down to Earth* (Grand Rapids, MI: Eerdmans, 1980), p. 178
8   Nancy Freund, "Costas to 'Invade' Costa Rica Soon," [unknown newspaper from Costas archive] (1969/70), p. 5
9   *Ibid.*
10 Costas, "Conversion," p. 180

political ones."[11] This conversion to the world not only served him in the Hispanic ghettoes of America but also in Latin America. Costas moved to Costa Rica to begin a decade-long term of service as a missionary under the auspices of the Latin American Mission and the United Church Board for World Ministries.[12] Significantly, he was commissioned[13] at the very church[14] that Adoniram Judson, the first American missionary, had been commissioned in nearly 170 years prior.[15]

And finally, the fourth conversion was the conversion to Macedonia. After a decade of service in Latin America, Orlando felt the call back to the U.S., likening it to the Apostle Paul's call to Macedonia in Acts 16, "when, according to the tradition, the Christian faith passed into the European world."[16] Thus he returned to the United States, an area which he had written prophetically about several years before:

Can the nation with the greatest missionary presence in the world be regarded "a mission field"? If so, can that sector of the world which represents the habitat of the have-nots and the oppressed of the earth have anything to contribute to the missionary situation of the USA? ... The USA qualifies as "a mission field" because many of its people are alienated from God and neighbour. In spite of the millions who profess to be Christians by virtue of baptism, church membership or conventionality, an overwhelming number of North Americans have not *really heard* the gospel nor had a reasonable opportunity to consider it as a *personal* option. They go through life without a personal awareness of the God who in creation and redemption has staked a claim upon their lives and invites them to experience, by the power of his Spirit, freedom, community and hope. The dominant systems of this situation of alienation are fear, anxiety,

---

11 Costas, "Conversion," p. 181
12 "Orlando E. Costas 1942-1987," *Today's Ministry: A Report from Andover Newton,* Vol. V, Issue 2, (Newton Centre, MA: Andover Newton Theological School, Winter 1988), p. 3
13 on 20 October 1976.
14 Tabernacle Church, Salem, Massachusetts, USA.
15 Orlando Costas, "On Being a Missionary in the Last Quarter of the Twentieth Century," *Occasional Essays,* December 1976. In another link to Judson, Costas would later become the Adoniram Judson Professor of Missiology at Andover Newton Theological School.
16 *Ibid.*

distrust, at the personal level, and racism, inequality and exploitation at the social level. The USA also qualifies as a mission field because the witness of North American Christians is intrinsically related to their life and thought as a church and as an indissoluble part of their culture and society. Whatever they do affects their missionary activity at home and abroad. Whatever happens in the North American socio-cultural milieu affects the life and thought of the North American church. This, in turn, affects the life and thought of churches abroad, especially their own missionary witness, and the fulfilment of the *missio politica oecumenica* noted above.[17]

These four conversions of Orlando Costas can be paradigmatic for several reasons. First of all, conversion to Christ is primary and foremost. Without that as a foundation, we cannot even call ourselves Christians and have no basis for even speaking about other conversions. Without Christ, any other conversion is nothing more than secular humanism or social activism. But we ought not to stop there. Although we should not make the mistake of thinking that the other conversions are as important as conversion to Christ, we should also not make the opposite mistake of thinking that conversion to Christ is the end all and be all. This sometimes is the claim of those who espouse a "classical" Western theology removed from any culture whatsoever.

And so, the second conversion of Costas was his conversion to culture. As non-Western Christianity has shown us, culture is very important. In fact, Christianity cannot be conveyed apart from culture. Even something as simple as the statement "Jesus is Lord" has cultural implications. What does the word "Lord" mean to someone who doesn't live in a feudal or monarchic society? Or the word "God" could imply ancestral spirits to some cultures. I once had a conversation with a Pakistani Muslim and he made the observation that Islam adapts the culture to the religion, whereas Christianity adapts the religion to the culture. In other words, where Islam goes, Sharia law is imposed, the Arabic language is imposed, mandatory public call to prayer five times a day is imposed, in short, the culture is adapted to the religion. Where Christianity goes, the Bible is translated into the

---

17 Orlando Costas, "The USA: A Mission Field for Third World Christians?" *Review and Expositor*, Vol. LXXIV, No. 2, Spring 1977, pp. 183-4

vernacular, local worship styles and music are used, and sometimes Scripture has even helped to preserve the local language by giving it a written form, in short, the religion is adapted to the culture. The one major exception to this rule is the Catholic Church, which up until recently has insisted that Latin be used instead of the vernacular. But since Vatican II that is no longer an issue, and even the Catholic Church is changing. In this increasingly multi-ethnic and multi-cultural world we live in, globalism can creep in and threaten to drive out cultural differences. But cultural differences should be celebrated as vehicles for conveying God's grace. As John Piper has said, "[The] beauty and power of praise that will come to the Lord from the diversity of the nations are greater than the beauty and power that would come to him if the chorus of the redeemed were culturally uniform."[18]

Orlando Costas's third conversion was his conversion to the world. He called himself a "radical evangelical" which means an evangelical Christian who takes seriously the Bible and orthodox theology, but also integrates it with the demands of Scripture in orthopraxis and social justice. It's not just right thinking, but right action. Increasingly, evangelicals are becoming re-aware of this side of the gospel. In fact, the word "radical" really means returning to the "roots." A square root of a number is also known as a radical. I'm not sure when the word "radical" lost its original meaning and came to mean something quite the opposite – extremism – but Costas saw himself merely as returning to the roots of Christianity, where social activism was a natural outflow of one's faith. The Lausanne movement of 1974 was established for the purpose of bridging orthodoxy with orthopraxis. The neo-evangelicalism of Billy Graham and Carl F.H. Henry was also an attempt at bringing a conciliar mentality to evangelicalism, working with social prophets like Martin Luther King, Jr. And this radical evangelical tradition stretches back quite a way to the tradition of the Anabaptists in the Radical Reformation, up until the present day with the Mennonites and people like Jim Wallis and *Sojourners* magazine. Costas was by no means alone in this vein; he stands in a tradition that is gradually re-awakening in the consciousness of this world's evangelicals. David Bebbington defines the four marks of an evangelical as someone who

---

18   John Piper, *Let the Nations Be Glad!* (Grand Rapids, MI: Baker Books, 1993), p. 216

is 1) conversionist; 2) Biblicist; 3) crucicentrist; and 4) activist.[19] Most evangelicals would agree with the first three but not necessarily the last one, but increasingly the "activist" side is becoming reintegrated. Philip Jenkins affirms this:

> "For the Left, the rise of the South suggests that Northern Christians must commit themselves firmly to social and political activism at home, to ensuring economic justice and combating racism, to promoting cultural diversity. Conservatives, in contrast, emphasize the moral and sexual conservatism of the emerging churches, and seek to enlist them as natural allies... For both sides, the new South is useful, politically and rhetorically...[20]

Finally, Costas's fourth conversion, the conversion to Macedonia, is becoming a reality. Third World Christians are becoming missionaries to the Western world. Continuing on, he says, "We can even imagine Southern Christians taking the initiative to the extent of evangelizing the North, in the process changing many familiar aspects of belief and practice, and exporting cultural traits presently found only in Africa or Latin America."[21] Globalization is not only going one way now; it's not merely the McDonaldization of the world, but maybe also the Africization or Asianization of the world. Costas was aware of this fact in the 1970s; he made it his goal to return to Macedonia, that is, to be a Third World missionary preaching to the great nation of the U.S.A. As Jenkins quoted: "Who should be missionaries to whom?"[22]

The Significance of Orlando Costas: A Latino Paradigm for the Next Christendom

Orlando Costas is significant for several reasons. First of all, because he is Latino, he represents not only the fastest-growing minority population in the United States, but also the most Christianized continent on earth. A recent online article on MSN stated that the 41.3 million Hispanics in the U.S. comprise one-seventh of the total population and are growing at a 3.7% annual rate, as compared to an average of 1% for the rest of the American

---

19 David Bebbington, *Evangelicalism in Modern Britain* (London: Unwin Hyman, 1989), pp. 2-19
20 Philip Jenkins, *The Next Christendom* (Oxford: Oxford University Press, 2002), p. 14
21 *Ibid.*
22 *Ibid.*, p. 204

population.[23]   Some major cities in the U.S. already have more Hispanics than any other group. For example, according to the 2000 census, Los Angeles is 45% Hispanic, 31% white, 12% Asian, and 9% black. The names of the four largest cities in California show that it was Mexico, not the United States, which first owned California. From smallest to largest, the four biggest cities are: San Francisco, San Jose, San Diego, and Los Angeles. In fact, the full name of L.A. is "La Ciudad de Nuestra Señora, La Reina de Los Angeles" (The City of Our Lady, Queen of the Angels). The new mayor of Los Angeles, Antonio Villaraigosa, was elected recently on 17 May 2005. He is the city's first Hispanic mayor since 1872. Perhaps L.A. actually doesn't stand for Los Angeles, but rather Latin America! But this phenomenon is not just in California; states like New York, Texas, New Mexico, and Illinois already have significant Hispanic populations.

But Orlando Costas was not just a Hispanic American, he was Puerto Rican which meant that his roots were Caribbean and Spanish. The mix of Spaniards, African slaves, and the indigenous Indians have contributed to a cultural and racial mix that remains to this day, denoted by the word *mestizaje*.[24] In a recent movie called *Los Diarios de Motocicleta* (The Motorcycle Diaries), a young Che Guevara makes a speech calling for a united America, saying that "We are one single *mestizo* race, from Mexico all the way down to the straits of Magellan." Perhaps this is a bit idealistic, but the reality of miscegenation is an advantage that no other continent on the world shares except for Latin America. Also, Philip Jenkins points out that Puerto Rico would be the most Protestant nation of Latin America if it were its own separate country,[25] so perhaps it's not so surprising that one of Latin America's most vocal *evangélicos*[26] should come from Puerto Rico.

The fact of Orlando's Hispanic heritage should serve not to exclude others, but rather to encourage. He exemplified interlocution at its best by befriending people of all backgrounds, ethnicities, and nationalities. The former president of Andover Newton Theological School, George Peck, remarked:

---

23 10 June 2005, see: http://www.msnbc.msn.com/id/8147476/?GT1=6657
24 López, p. 482
25 Jenkins, p. 61
26 In Latin America, all Protestants, whether they be evangelical, mainline, Pentecostal, independent, etc. are known as *evangélicos*.

[T]here was, of course, [Costas's] almost legendary *relationship with the church around the world.* Have you ever realized how many people Orlando knew, and in how many places? He was a "world person" as very few people are. There were times when I was convinced he literally knew everyone.[27]

If we could do even half as well as Orlando in reaching out to the worldwide body of Christ, the church would probably be in a much better place.

As an ethnic minority, Orlando Costas was accepted in places where Anglos may not be accepted. And yet he earned four academic degrees, including a doctorate in theology from the Free University of Amsterdam. Again, this study of Costas is one of *being* and *thinking,* an ontological and epistemological blend. He had the best education the West could offer, combined with his emergence as an important Christian leader in the non-Western world.

The Theology of Orlando Costas: Evangelization from the Periphery

Orlando Costas's writings contain many themes, but one of the most striking is his theology of "Christ outside the gate." He takes this idea from Hebrews 13:12 which says: "So Jesus also suffered outside the gate in order to sanctify the people through his own blood."[28] What more appropriate chord can be struck among people of the Next Christendom? The very Lord that we serve is one of us. Not only did Jesus take human form to dwell among us, *Immanuel,* but he died as an outcast, outside the city gate, with not even a place of honour. Costas writes:

> With Jesus there came a fundamental shift in the location of salvation: the centre was moved to the periphery. Jesus died in the wilderness among the outcast and disenfranchised. The unclean and defiled territory became holy ground as he took upon himself the function of the temple. With the change of location came also a shift in focus. The concept of salvation was now seen in a broader and more radical perspective. No longer was it understood in terms of a mere benefit. The focus was now on commitment to a life of service. Jesus died "to

---

27   George Peck, "President's Column," *Today's Ministry,* Winter 1988, p. 2
28   Orlando Costas, *Christ Outside the Gate* (Maryknoll, NY: Orbis, 1982), p. 188

sanctify the people," that is, to set them apart for ministry... Salvation means, in other words, freedom to confess Jesus Christ in the service of outsiders.[29]

Although, it must be said, Costas would have probably eschewed the nomenclature of "The Next Christendom" because he was not thrilled with the word "Christendom." He thought it too strongly implied a division between the privileged people and the outcasts. The old adage of the church fathers, "Outside of the church there is no salvation," can be abused to divide the insiders from the outsiders, i.e. those who don't look like the Western church can have no salvation.[30] But what happens when it is the outsiders who become the new Christendom? Many people accuse the New Testament of being anti-Semitic, and honestly it probably is. But the context was different back then, because the Jews and Romans were in power, and they were persecuting the Christian minority. And minorities feel a need to speak out against their oppressors. So the New Testament polemic was both anti-Jewish and anti-Roman. The problem lies in the historical advent of Christendom. After Constantine, Christians were no longer in the minority. But Christendom continued to use the texts that the first century minority Christians used, and suddenly the same Scripture that once upheld the oppressed became like the proverbial bull in a china shop, wreaking havoc everywhere it touches by people who wield their power carelessly. Philip Jenkins points out that "Southern Christianity today stands in much the same relationship to the wider society that the church did in the Roman Empire, before and after the great age of conversions."[31] So what happens when Christendom shifts to the non-Western world? Suddenly those who had no power become the majority. It is well and good in one sense: the plight of the poor and oppressed will now be heard, as they are now the majority voice. But let us offer a caveat if we do not want the vices of the Old Christendom to be visited upon the New Christendom. Perhaps another Christendom should not be what we are after. Costas would remind us that Jesus's death outside the city gate of Jerusalem is a salvation that frees us for service rather than a "ticket to a privileged spot in God's universe."[32]

---

29 *Ibid.*, p. 189
30 *Ibid.*, pp. 189-90
31 Jenkins, pp. 134-5
32 Costas, *Gate*, p. 191

Another theme that Costas frequently developed is the idea of "evangelization from the periphery," using Galilee as a model. He takes this theological idea from the Gospel of Mark. Costas says that Galilee is a key not only to understanding Mark but to unlocking Jesus's evangelistic legacy.[33] He points out that Jesus used Galilee, not Jerusalem, as his headquarters. The significance of Galilee lay in the fact that it was not only far removed from the centre of Jewish power, but it was also a multiethnic area full of undesirables, so much so that even the Jews there were considered outcasts.[34] Jesus took his place among the "nobodies" in order to make them "somebodies".[35] Costas points out three factors about Galilee: 1) Galilee was Jesus's base, so that he not only ministered to the poor, oppressed, and outcast, but he recruited them to be his first followers. So he ministered *to* them and ministered *from* them. So often Western missions go *to* the non-Western world, but rarely do they try to minister *from* their perspective. 2) Galilee represents the public multitudes. In every place in the world, one can find "Galileans" who are "the powerless, the marginalized, and the voiceless."[36] Ministering publicly to them will send ripples to Jerusalem, the centres of power. 3) Galilee also represents more than just the powerless in our midst, but a larger worldwide evangelistic endeavour. To stay in our own enclaves is selfish; we are mandated by the Great Commission to go to the ends of the earth. But in every nation, the peripheral people should be the ones targeted. To attempt a top-down approach is to end up with a privatized gospel and a "plastic Jesus."[37] The grassroots is the fundamental point of reference in evangelization, according to Costas. Only from there can the gospel be a transforming force.

INFEMIT

Orlando Costas made some controversial moves in his lifetime, and one of them was the formation of INFEMIT, the International Fellowship of Missions Theologians from the Two-Thirds World. This was controversial mainly because of its genesis rather than its substance. Costas was invited to participate in the 1974 Lausanne Congress for World Evangelization in Switzerland. In 1980, a second

---

33 Orlando Costas, *Liberating News* (Grand Rapids, MI: Eerdmans, 1989), p. 49
34 *Ibid.*, p. 50
35 *Ibid.*, pp. 52-3
36 *Ibid.*, p. 64
37 *Ibid.*, p. 69

Lausanne conference was held in Pattaya, Thailand. While there, he and other Third World theologians felt that the needs of the non-Western church were largely being ignored, that the world was quite different in 1980 as opposed to 1974, and Lausanne had not moved forward to keep pace with the times. These Third World theologians drafted a "protest paper"[38] which was signed by not a few participants in this conference. This paper essentially fell on deaf ears with the exception of one significant member of the Lausanne board: John Stott. But Stott was a lone voice crying in the wilderness. As a result, Costas and his colleagues broke off from Lausanne in order to accomplish what they believed was essential.[39] If the current vehicle for world evangelization was not doing its job, a new vehicle was needed.

Costas was not just a theologian, but a practitioner of his theology. He believed a modern-day Galilee was needed, and the perspective had to be from the periphery. So together with his friends Vinay Samuel from India and David Gitari from Kenya, he formed the International Fellowship of Missions Theologians. The purpose of INFEMIT was not just to build solidarity with Christians from the Two-Thirds World, but also because of the realization that "if non-white, non-Western theologians were going to be heard by the North Atlantic missiological establishment, they needed to talk among themselves and theologize together."[40] Costas saw this mandate as applicable not just to Christians in the Two- Thirds World, but also to Christians of ethnic minority status in the U.S.:

> [Costas] sets a missionary agenda for Third World Christians in North America: they can serve as a mirror for the critical self-understanding of American churches; they can offer models of authentic contextualization; they can provide meaningful paradigms of dynamic, liberating church leadership in contrast with the highly clericalized American church; and they can offer a partnership for radical discipleship.[41]

---

38 Costas was one of the primary authors of this paper, along with six others.

39 See Orlando Costas, "Proclaiming Christ in the Two Thirds World" in Vinay Samuel and Chris Sugden, eds., *Sharing Jesus in the Two Thirds World* (Oxford: OCMS, 1983).

40 Samuel Escobar, "The Legacy of Orlando Costas," *International Bulletin of Missionary Research* (New Haven, CT: Overseas Ministries Study Center, April 2001)., pp. 53-4

41 *Ibid.*, p. 55

INFEMIT originally began as an amalgamation of the Latin American Theological Fraternity, the African Theological Fraternity, and Partnership in Mission Asia. It eventually was expanded to include INFEMIT USA and INFEMIT Europe, with the support of men like Ron Sider and Peter Kuzmič, respectively. INFEMIT is also the parent organization that founded the Oxford Centre for Missions Studies. This organization exists to foster the theological voices from the Two Thirds World, the voices of the younger churches. It was founded in the early 1980s, when a group of theologians already saw the advent of the Next Christendom a quarter of a century ago.

It was not just the Western world which could not see the Christianity as Costas saw. Even within the Latin American Theological Fraternity, Orlando Costas encountered some opposition to this idea of INFEMIT. One of his colleagues, Samuel Escobar, wrote:

> Orlando tried to develop a bridge-building ministry through advocacy. He could not always convince all of us, his Latin American colleagues, that we should cross the borders he crossed. But we have to acknowledge the authenticity of his commitment to have fellowship and partnership with whoever shared his pressing sense of missionary obligation, regardless of ecclesiastical blocks and affiliations. This accounts for the recognition of his missiological work in a wide diversity of circles.[42]

Costas wanted *all* the so-called "Galileans" to work together. He desired for the Latin Americans to join forces with the Asians, the Africans, and those on the periphery in the U.S. and Europe. Right here in front of you, you have a living example of someone who Costas has affected. I am a Chinese man from the U.S., studying a Latin American in England. Costas saw that we cannot remain in our own parochialism but we must embrace each other and work together.

Conclusion

Although Philip Jenkins was not the first to recognize the shift of the centre of gravity of Christianity to the non-Western world, the world does owe him some credit for bringing this fact into the consciousnesses of a far wider audience than anyone has ever done before. Orlando Costas was a precursor to Jenkins, and he not only

---

42 Samuel Escobar, *Transformation*, July/September 1988.

wrote about the next Christendom but lived it out. He was converted fourfold – to Christ, to culture, to the world, and back to Macedonia. Costas put this into writing and emphasized the theology about Christ dying outside the gate for us, and the fact that Jesus used Galilee as his base and not Jerusalem. Costas put this theology of the periphery into action when he established the International Fellowship of Missions Theologians to give a voice to the theology of the rest of the world. Costas emphasized the periphery because he followed his God there. Or perhaps it was that Jesus came down to meet Costas where he already was. It's probably a bit of both, as Galilee was both where Christ came from and where he was going to. And it is true of the Next Christendom today: it is both where the majority of Christians now are from, but it's also where we are all going to.

Bibliography

David Bebbington, *Evangelicalism in Modern Britain: A History from the 1730s to the 1980s* (London: Unwin Hyman, 1989).

Dannette Costas, "Missiology: From the Underside of History" [interview with Dr. Orlando E. Costas], (Newton Centre, MA: 29 November 1985).

Orlando Costas, "On Being a Missionary in the Last Quarter of the Twentieth Century," *Occasional Essays*, December 1976.

_____, "The USA: A Mission Field for Third World Christians?" *Review and Expositor*, Vol. LXXIV, No. 2, Spring 1977.

_____, "Conversion as a Complex Experience—A Personal Case Study" in John R.W. Stott and Robert Coote, eds., *Down to Earth: Studies in Christianity and Culture* (Grand Rapids, MI: Eerdmans, 1980).

_____, "Proclaiming Christ in the Two Thirds World" in Vinay Samuel and Chris Sugden, eds., *Sharing Jesus in the Two Thirds World* (Oxford: OCMS, 1983).

_____, *Liberating News: A Theology of Contextual Evangelization* (Grand Rapids, MI: Eerdmans, 1989).

Samuel Escobar, *Transformation*, July/September 1988.

Nancy Freund, "Costas to 'Invade' Costa Rica Soon," [unknown newspaper from Costas archive] (1969/70).

Philip Jenkins, *The Next Christendom: The Coming of Global Christianity* (Oxford: Oxford University Press, 2002).

Adalberto López, *The Puerto Ricans: Their History, Culture, and Society* (Cambridge, MA: Schenkman Publishing Company, Inc., 1980).

George Peck, "President's Column," *Today's Ministry*, Winter 1988.

John Piper, *Let the Nations Be Glad! The Supremacy of God in Missions* (Grand Rapids, MI: Baker Books, 1993).

"Orlando E. Costas 1942-1987," *Today's Ministry: A Report from Andover Newton*, Vol. V, Issue 2, (Newton Centre, MA: Andover Newton Theological School, Winter 1988).

'NOT JUST US AND THEM' – INTER-FAITH IRELAND AND THE MISSIOLOGICAL IMPLICATIONS

Stephen Skuce

1. Ireland in binocular vision

For several hundred years it has been commonplace to consider that Ireland is composed of two related but distinct ethnic communities of which one of the defining characteristics is an inheritance of some form of Protestantism or Catholicism. It is clear that this has not always been the case, but since the Reformation in Europe and the significant plantations of Ireland by English and Scots settlers in the seventeenth century, this generalisation has had some validity. This generalisation has distinct political and missiological implications to this day.

Yet Ireland had a distinctive pre-Christian history with successive waves of migrants imposing their religious views on the indigenous population. For example, Newgrange, predating the Egyptian pyramids and rivalling them in religious sophistication, fell into misuse after the Celtic migration.[1]

Beyond that, Ireland has not remained aloof from the currents of faith swirling around the world for the past two millennia. That the story is not well known does not make it invalid, rather there is a need to rediscover inter-faith Ireland.

2. Historic inter-faith reality

St Patrick, his namesakes, his forerunners and subsequent evangelists found a sophisticated religious system in place. Tradition talks of power encounters between Patrick and Druids, of absorption of Celtic religious understanding and figures into what developed into Celtic Christianity but relatively little significant opposition, illustrated by the paucity of early Christian martyrs in Ireland.[2]

---

1 MacUistin, L., *Exploring Newgrange*, (Dublin: O'Brien Press, 1999).
2 O'Hogain, D., *The Celts: A History*, (Cork: Collins Press, 2002).

2:1 Vikings

When the first Viking longboats were sighted in 795AD the nominally Christian Irish would have looked in wonder, and then fairly rapidly in horror, as hordes of bearded warriors set about plundering the wealth of coastal Ireland.[3] When Vikings eventually began to settle they fairly quickly adopted Christianity and so the Irish Christianised a significant number of migrants, a wonderful missiological thought. What is not so wholesome is the thought that later waves of Viking invaders, raping and pillaging with gusto, were probably as Christian as most of the Irish in the ninth century.[4]

One consequence of the Viking attacks was to introduce the Irish to the whole range of world faiths then known to Europeans. Vikings captured slaves in Ireland, sold them on to Muslim slave dealers in the eastern Mediterranean who sold them as far east as north India. So the prospector with a metal detector today in Sweden can come across treasure trove dating to the ninth century and containing an Irish Celtic cross, a golden Buddha, Hindu gods and perhaps a copy of the Qu'ran.

2:2 Jews

Legends linking Ireland with the Jewish people in pre-Christian times include Noah's daughter sailing her ark here, Jeremiah establishing Brehon Law, the Puck Fair in Co Kerry being based on the scapegoat of Leviticus, and British Israelites spending millions (in today's values) searching for the Ark of the Covenant at Tara at the start of the twentieth century.[5]

The first documented visit by Jews to Ireland was in 1078 when the Annals of Innisfallen record five Jews visiting Turlough O'Brien but not getting much of a welcome. Amazingly Ireland was seriously mooted as a national homeland for the Jews in Cromwell's time – a plan that was considered to solve Europe's perceived 'Jewish problem' and England's 'Catholic problem'. World history would have taken a

---

3   Etchingham, C., *Viking Raids on Irish Church Settlements in the Ninth Century: A Reconsideration,* (Maynooth, St Patrick's College, Dept of Old and Middle Irish, 1996).
4   Carver, M. (ed), *The Cross Goes North: Processes of Conversion in Northern Europe, AD300-1300,* (York: York Medieval Press, 2003).
5   Siev, S., *The Celts and Hebrews,* (Dublin: The Irish Jewish Museum, 1995), Carnew, M., *Tara and the Ark of the Covenant,* (Dublin: The Royal Irish Academy, 2003).

very different course had this been adopted. The further Irish Jewish interaction has been well documented.[6]

Irish churches have never significantly engaged with Ireland's small Jewish population, which only significantly grew in the late nineteenth century and peaked around 8,000 in the late 1950s. Whilst Irish Presbyterianism had a long organised missionary outreach to Jews in Germany and North Africa, they never attempted a similar work in Ireland. There has been little anti-Semitism in Ireland. However the Limerick Pogrom of 1904 and the Irish government response to appeals to take in refugee Jews during WWII illustrate that this was only relative to most of the rest of Europe.[7]

2:3 Muslims

The positive 18th century experiences of Dean Mahomet, an exotic character who went on to run bath houses in Brighton frequented by the British royalty, belies any long term Islamophobic attitude in Ireland.[8] Irish people's early involvement with Muslims was largely through pilgrimage to the Holy Land and some trading links. There had been very little Irish involvement in the crusades although violent confrontation was not absent. Irish shores were very occasionally raided by Muslim pirates with the Sack of Baltimore in 1631, immortalised in song by Thomas Davis, the most memorable incident when 200 Irish were taken as slaves.

Muslim migration into Ireland in a very recent phenomena, largely originating with post WWII students, mostly medical, to Dublin. While numbers have grown rapidly in the last ten years to over 30,000 in Ireland it is of note that Ireland's main initial experience of Islam in Ireland was through well educated, articulate and generally wealthy individuals.

2:4 Hindus

Ireland still has a relatively small Hindu population but the Irish nationalist influence on Indian nationalism has been well documented. There have been fascinating individuals resident in Ireland such as the

---

6   See Hyman, L., *The Jews of Ireland: from Earliest Times to the Year 1910*, (Shannon: Irish University Press, 1972) and Keogh, D., *Jews in Twentieth Century Ireland*, (Cork: Cork University Press, 1998).
7   There are many anti-Semitic incidents that are detailed in the works previously cited and while not on the scale of other European countries are not to be minimised.
8   Fisher, M., 'Cork's Dean Mahomet' in *Journal of the Cork Historical and Archaeological Society*, Vol 101 (1996).

Maharajah of Connemara in the 1920s.[9] The early Irish - Hindu interaction was during British colonial days in India. While it's not surprising that many of the Anglo-Irish worked as administrators and army officers in India, the role of Irish Catholics is not so well recognised. At a time when Catholics could not officially serve in the British army, India was ruled by the British East India Company and their militia, not formally the British army, at times comprised 40% Irish Catholic membership.

General Sir John Nicholson from Dungannon is one of the few Irishmen to have a Hindu cult in his honour. The Nicholsonians were an obscure group attracted to this Victorian 'hero' figure. They never numbered many but made enough of an impact that when the Indian government were removing Nicholson's statue from Delhi in the 1950s an armed guard was posted in case remnants of this cult took exception.[10]

2:5 Irish abroad

Whether as British soldiers or administrators, emigrants or missionaries, or modern day business people, backpackers and aid workers, Irish people have had a long and fascinating and ongoing engagement with people of other faith. Space does not permit documenting the various approaches but since Ireland never had any colonies of her own, some of the worst colonial excesses have been avoided, placing Ireland in a positive inter-faith position today, unsaddled by the legacy of colonial history. That said, there is a case for looking at Montserrat as equating to an Irish colony and there is enough evidence to show there that the Irish, given a chance, would have acted as badly as any other colonial group.[11] However, apart from the involvement with Britain, Ireland does not have a history of poor interaction with people of other faiths, be it through crusades, pogroms or colonial exploitation.

9   Chambers, A., *Ranji: Maharajah of Connemara*, (Dublin: Wolfhound Press, 2002).

10 Kapur, N., *The Irish Raj: Illustrated Stories about the Irish in India and Indians in Ireland*, (Antrim: Greystone Press, 1996).

11 Akenson, D.H., *If the Irish Ran the World: Montserrat 1630-1730*, (Liverpool: Liverpool University Press, 1997).

1   Contemporary Ireland

2002 Irish Census Religious Denomination	Persons
Roman Catholic	3,462,606
Church of Ireland(inc. Protestant)	115,611
Christian (unspecified)	21,403
Presbyterian	20,582
Muslim (Islamic)	19,147
Orthodox	10,437
Methodist	10,033
Jehovah's Witness	4,430
Buddhist	3,894
Evangelical	3,780
Apostolic or Pentecostal	3,152
Hindu	3,099
Lutheran	3,068
Baptist	2,265
Jewish	1,790
Pantheist	1,106
Agnostic	1,028
Quaker (Society of Friends)	859
Latter Day Saints (Morman)	833
Lapsed Roman Catholic	590
Atheist	500
Baha'I	490
Brethren	222
Other stated religions	8,920
No religion	138,264
Not stated	79,094
Total	3,917,203

Source   www.cso.ie

Population of Jews in the Republic of Ireland

	1861	1871	1881	1891	1901	1911	1926	1936	1946
State	341	230	394	1,506	3,006	3,805	3,686	3,749	3,907

1961	1971	1981	1991	2002
3,255	2,633	2,127	1,581	1,790

Population of those other than Christians and Jews in the Republic of Ireland

	1861	1871	1881	1891	1901	1911	1926	1936
State	11,820	18,990	12,560	11,399	11,696	11,913	9,730	8,005

	1946	1961	1971	1981	1991	2002
	8,113	5,236	6,248	10,843	38,743	89,223

Northern Ireland Population	1991		2001	
Religion	**Number**	**%**	**Number**	**%**
Catholic	605,639	38.40%	678,462	40.26%
Presbyterian	336,891	21.40%	348,742	20.69%
Church of Ireland	279,280	17.70%	257,788	15.30%
Methodist	59,517	3.80%	59,173	3.51%
Baptist	19,484	1.20%	*	*
Brethren	12,446	0.80%	*	*
Congregationalist	8,176	0.50%	*	*
Unitarian	3,213	0.20%	*	.*
Other	79,129	5.00%	102,211[1]	6.07%
Other Religions	*	*	5,082[2]	0.33%
None	59,234	3.70%	*	*
Not Stated	114,827	7.30%	233,853[3]	13.88%
Total	1,577,836	100.00%	1,685,267	100.00%

Source: Northern Ireland Census 2001

Notes: * Figures not available, **1.** Other Christian (including Christian related), **2.** Other religions and philosophies, **3.** Persons with no religion or religion not stated

Northern Ireland population

Year	Total popl'n	Other Denominations		None		Not stated	
		Number	**%**	**Number**	**%**	**Number**	**%**
1861	1,396,453	18,646	1.3			445	0.1
1871	1,359,190	32,816	2.4			387	0.0
1881	1,304,816	40,317	3.1			1,527	0.1
1891	1,236,056	41,958	3.4			2,005	0.2
1901	1,236,952	47,971	3.9			1,070	0.1
1911	1,250,531	49,827	4.0			2,486	0.2
1926	1,256,561	52,177	4.1			2,304	0.2
1937	1,279,745	57,541	4.5			2,374	0.2
1951	1,370,921	63,497	4.6			5,865	0.4
1961	1,425,042	71,299	5.0			26,418	1.9
1971	1,519,540	87,838	5.8			142,511	18.5
1981	1,481,959	112,822	7.6			274,584	18.5
1991	1,577,836	122,448	7.8	58,234	3.7	114,827	7.3

Source: The Northern Ireland Census 1991: Religion Report

The statistics show a pattern of increasing non-Christian populations in both Northern Ireland and the Republic of Ireland. Consequently an increasing exposure to and interaction with other faith communities by the host Christian background community is apparent. Other statistics show the rise of racist attacks in Northern Ireland.

4. Inter-faith bodies

The first inter-faith body in Ireland was the short lived Pillar of Fire Society, founded by Frank Duff in Dublin in 1942, bringing together Catholics, Protestants and Jews in theological debate. This group, similar in many ways to its contemporary Mercier Society, was closed by Cardinal McQuaid, due to his unease at Catholic doctrine being expounded by lay Catholics.

The Council of Christians and Jews (Ireland), part of an international movement, was established in Dublin in 1981, under the encouragement of the Sisters of Zion, a Catholic order devoted to Christian – Jewish understanding. A sister organisation was founded in Belfast in 1996.

The Northern Ireland Inter-Faith Forum was formed in Belfast in 1993 largely through the work of Revd Maurice Ryan. This comprehensive group has representatives from almost all of Northern Ireland's religious communities and has played a significant role in providing multi religious educational materials. The inter-faith chapel at Belfast International airport came about through initiatives from this group. The Dublin Three Faiths Forum, with representation from the Christian, Jewish and Muslim communities, was established in 1997 and seeks to promote understanding and mutual awareness between the respective communities.

5. Missiological Implications

There are a number of missiological implications resulting from this brief analysis of the emerging Irish inter-faith context.

5:1 Mission in a multi-faith context

Mission no longer involves just those nominally associated with one's 'own side'. While residence along religiously segregated lines is an enduring feature of Northern Irish life, those who are Muslims, Hindus and Jews reside in numerous areas, although many locate close by respective places of worship.

Local communities throughout Ireland now include people of various faiths and while they do not constitute a very significant overall number, in all Irish cities and in increasing numbers of towns, other faith communities are increasing realities. Therefore mission needs a multi-faith focus. Just how this is worked out will depend on the group engaged in mission and their local context, but increasingly multi-faith issues will come into play.

5:2 Freedom of worship

Northern Ireland has a recent history of sectarian attacks on Christian places of worship. There have been a small number of incidents affecting some of Ireland's synagogues but these generally have been aberrant individual actions not indicative of any systematic opposition. However the Muslim community in Craigavon has recently encountered significant opposition to the establishment of a mosque. Here the Christian community have an opportunity to stand up for what has long been considered a feature of Protestantism – freedom of worship. Part of the mission of Christianity in Ireland, and especially that of evangelicalism, needs to be agitation for freedom of worship and religious rights for Ireland's religious minorities. It is within memory in the Republic of Ireland when boycotts of protestant communities brought significant economic and social hardship. Here is an opportunity to engage creatively and helpfully with a portion of Ireland's Muslim community.

5:3 Shared social concerns

Ireland's Christians have traditionally taken conservative stances on a variety of social issues. Potentially they have a new ally, if they have the courage to take this emerging mission opportunity. Only occasionally have Protestants and Catholics been united on social issues, an anti abortion position being a generally common cause. Ireland's Muslims, despite many internal differences that are not always recognised by the wider community, can be strong allies in issues related to alcohol abuse. They hold a position on alcohol similar to that traditionally maintained by Methodism. This is but one example of a number of areas where Christians and people of other faiths can unite in common cause. Given the Muslim aversion for secularism, and that secularism in its many forms is one of the main forces opposing traditional Christian values, there are both macro and micro issues where a common faith approach would be both appropriate and useful.

5:4 Contextual inter-faith reflection

Ireland has produced very few significant contextual theologians. There are many significant Irish theologians, with Alister McGrath the contemporary towering figure and CS Lewis that of a previous generation. Both share a similarity of Irish background but of third level education and subsequent professional career outside of Ireland. Neither has written as Irish people reflecting on the Irish context.

It may be optimistic, but the emerging inter-faith context of Ireland may provoke some of Ireland's theological and missiological thinkers to reflect on the new reality. It is a task that can really only be done by Irish in Ireland. Borrowing insights from England, America or Europe will not be sufficient to address the specific Irish context. Our broadly evangelical theological colleges should be places producing some of this material.

5:5 Mission engaging other faith communities abroad

Irish of all Christian traditions have been very willing participants in the eighteenth to twentieth century western missionary project. That project is largely coming to an end as indigenous Christians communities are found in almost every nation and as Christianity declines in Europe and Ireland finds itself the destination for missionaries rather than the point of departure.

Given the Irish enthusiasm for evangelising Hindus, Buddhist and Muslims abroad, the new reality is that Ireland now has its own Hindu, Buddhist and Muslim communities. The responsibility to evangelise other faith communities now rests on the Irish in Ireland. Our days of going as evangelists to Africa, India and elsewhere are largely, although not completely, over. But where are the emerging organisations to do this work in Ireland? Why are the Home Mission departments of the mainstream Protestant denominations not engaged in this task? That it needs to be done with love, compassion, sensitivity and understanding goes without saying. But it needs to be done.

5. Conclusion

A look at the new Ireland requires us to reconsider how we do mission. Old methods and attitudes may have worked in their day, but that day is passing, if not already passed. We need to engage in Ireland as it is, not as it was. Maybe our overseas missionary engagement was but a preparation for our greater contribution towards the evangelisation of Africa, India etc, that contribution being a positive evangelistic engagement with the other faith communities in Ireland, with the ripples of that truly going from Jerusalem and Judea to Samaria and the ends of the earth.

Select Bibliography

Akenson, D.H., *If the Irish Ran the World: Montserrat 1630-1730,* Liverpool: Liverpool University Press, 1997

Carnew, M., *Tara and the Ark of the Covenant,* Dublin: The Royal Irish Academy, 2003

Carver, M. (ed), *The Cross Goes North: Processes of Conversion in Northern Europe, AD300-1300,* York: York Medieval Press, 2003

Chambers, A., *Ranji: Maharajah of Connemara,* Dublin: Wolfhound Press, 2002

Etchingham, C., *Viking Raids on Irish Church Settlements in the Ninth Century: A Reconsideration,* Maynooth, St Patrick's College, Dept of Old and Middle Irish, 1996

Fisher, M., 'Cork's Dean Mahomet' in *Journal of the Cork Historical and Archaeological Society,* Vol 101 (1996).

Hyman, L., *The Jews of Ireland: From earliest Times to 1910,* Shannon: Irish University Press, 1972

Kapur, N., *The Irish Raj: Illustrated Stories about the Irish in India and Indians in Ireland,* Antrim: Greystone Press, 1996

Keogh, D., *The Jews in Twentieth Century Ireland,* Cork: Cork University Press, 1998

MacUistin, L., *Exploring Newgrange,* Dublin: O'Brien Press, 1999

O'Hogain, D., *The Celts: A History,* Cork: Collins Press, 2002

Siev, S., *The Celts and Hebrews,* Dublin: The Irish Jewish Museum, 1995

SELECT BIBLIOGRAPHY

C. Allen, *The Buddha and the Sahibs* (John Murray, 2002)

Allan Anderson, *An Introduction to Pentecostalism* (CUP, 2004)

E. Barker and M. Warburg (eds.), *New Religions and New Religiosity* (Aarhus, 1998)

K. Bediako, *Christianity in Africa: the renewal of a non-Western Religion* (Edinburgh University Press, 1995)

Callum Brown, *The Death of Christian Britain* (Routledge, 2001)

Judith Brown, *Christian Cultural Interactions and Indian Religious Traditions* (Eerdman's, 2002)

S. Bruce, *God is dead: secularisation in the West* (Blackwell, Oxford, 2002)

P. Cruchley-Jones, *Singing the Lord's song in a strange land?* (Peter Lang, Frankfurt, 2001)

Grace Davie, *Europe: the exceptional case* (DLT, 2002)

Grace Davie, *Religion in Modern Europe: a memory mutates* (OUP, 2000)

V. Fabiella and R.S. Sugirtharajah (eds.), *Dictionary of Third World Theologies* (SCM, 2003)

R.E. Frykenberg, *Christians and Missionaries in India: cross cultural communications since 1950* (Eerdman's, 2003)

C. Fyfe and A.F. Walls (eds.), *Christianity in Africa in the 1990's* (Edinburgh Centre of African Studies, 1996)

Robin Gill, *The "Empty" Church revisited* (Ashgate, 2003)

F. Halliday, *Islam and the Myth of Confrontation* (I.B. Tauris, London, 1996)

L. Halman and O. Riis, *Religion in Secularising Society* (Brill, Leiden, 2003)

R. Hedlund and B.J. Bhakaraj (eds.), *Missiology for the 21st Century: South Asian Perspectives* (ISPCK, New Delhi, 2004)

Samuel Huntingdon, *The Clash of Civilisations and the Remaking of World Order* (Touchstone Books, 1998)

Philip Jenkins, *The Next Christianity: the coming of global Christianity* (OUP, 2002)

D. Keogh, *The Jews in Twentieth Century Ireland* (Cork UP, 1998)

O. Kalu, *Power, Poverty and Prayer* (Peter Lang, Frankfurt, 2000)

R. King, *Orientalism and Religion: post-colonial theory, India and the "mystic east"* (Routledge, 1999)

D. Maclaren, *Mission Impossible: restoring credibility to the Church* (Paternoster, 2004)

T. Madan, *Modern Myths, locked minds: secularism and fundamentalism in India* (OUP, Delhi, 1998)

A.E. McGrath, *The Future of Christianity* (Blackwell, Oxford, 2002)

H. McLeod, *Secularisation in Western Europe 1848-1914* (Macmillan, 2000)

H. McLeod and W. Ustorf (eds.), *The Decline of Christendom in Western Europe* 1750-2000 (CUP, 2003)

Viigo Mortensen (ed.), *Theology and the Religions: a dialogue* (Eerdman's, 2003)

S. Murray, *Post Christendom* (Paternoster, 2004)

O. O'Donovan, *The Desire of the Nations: recovering the roots of political theology* (CUP, 1996)

D. O'Hogain, *The Celts: a history* (Collins Press, Cork, 2002)

Lamin Sanneh, *Translating the Message: the missionary impact on Culture* (Orbis, 1992)

Lamin Sanneh, *Whose religion is Christianity? The Gospel beyond the West* (Eerdman's, 2003)

L. Sanneh and J. Carpenter (eds.), *The Changing Face of Christianity: Africa, the West and the World* (OUP, New York, 2005)

R. Schreiter, *Reconciliation: mission and ministry in a changing social order* (Orbis, 1992)

David Smith, *Hinduism and Modernity* (Blackwell, Oxford, 2003)

David Smith, *Against the Stream: Christianity and Mission in an age of Globalization* (IVP, 2003)

Brian Stanley (ed.), *Christian Missions and the Enlightenment* (Eerdman's, 2001)

D. Tacey, *The Spirituality Revolution: the emergence of contemporary spirituality* (Harper Collins, Australia, 2003)

S. Taylor, *The Out of Bounds Church* (Zondervan, 2005)

P. van der Veer, *Imperial Encounters: religion and modernity in India and Britain* (Princeton UP, 2001)

A.F. Walls, *The Missionary Movement in Modern History: studies in the transmission of the faith* (Orbis, 1996)

World Christian Encyclopedia: a comprehensive survey of churches and religions in the modern world (OUP, New York, 2001)

K. Zebiri, *Muslims and Christians face to face* (One World, Oxford, 1997)

MISSION
- AN INVITATION TO GOD'S FUTURE
Edited by
Timothy Yates

Papers by Jürgen Moltmann, Theo Sundermeier, Christopher Rowland
and Anton Wessels

What is the shape of the Christian mission to be in the 21st century?

This is an especially pressing question in Europe, which appears to be increasingly de-Christianised.   In this collection of papers, some of the leading thinkers on mission in Europe address such issues as the theological foundation for mission, the place of dialogue with other faiths, the use of the arts in the cause of mission and questions of post-modernity.

"Exactly the kind of theological writing which can inspire the ministerial practitioner" *Expository Times*

"Essential*" Missiology*

"Addresses issues of real concern to ministers and churches" *Regent's Review*

"Good food for a new century" *Theology*

ISBN 1 898362 25 4

PUBLISHING
2000

A companion volume to
MISSION and SPIRITUALITY
CREATIVE WAYS OF BEING CHURCH

MISSION

and SPIRITUALITY

CREATIVE WAYS OF BEING CHURCH

Edited by

Howard Mellor & Timothy Yates

Papers by David Hay, Saunders Davies, Robert Kaggwa,
Brian Stanley, Pete Ward, Laurenti Magesa, Michael Crowley,
Esther de Waal, John Burgess, Craig Gardiner

How will the church be shaped to meet the needs of the 21st century?
In this collection, contributors from Britain, Tanzania, Uganda and
Latin America reflect on creative ways of being church in the
challenging contexts of post-modern society: and on what can be
learned from the spiritual traditions of the past to provide an inner
dynamic matched to the future.

'This collection is better than a curate's egg: all the parts are
good .... a thought provoking "must-have" for all who share
passion for mission and evangelism of any kind today'*Anvil*

ISBN 1 898362 28 9

2002

A companion volume to

MISSION
AN INVITATION TO GOD'S FUTURE

MISSION
VIOLENCE and
RECONCILIATION

Edited by

Howard Mellor and Timothy Yates

Papers by Robert Schreiter, Cecelia Clegg, David Porter,
Drew Gibson, Kenneth Ross, Margaret Raven, Jacques Matthey,
Kenneth Fleming, Andrew Wingate.

In a world plagued by violence, this collection examines the key issues relating to the way Christian mission can become both a peace-making and reconciling agency. The question is addressed by authors with particular insights from their own context in Africa, Nicaragua and Northern Ireland. The book also contains a masterly overview of the place of reconciliation as a key element of the Church's overall mission. Reconciliation and justice in dealing with violence, almost always a painful process, must be part of a mature way of dealing with these issues in the third millennium. This book explores how and why, and as such is a vital tool in considering the issues of cross cultural mission.

'an outstandingly valuable primer on a key subject for our time.... good reading!' *Theology*

'highly recommended to anyone who is interested in mission and reconciliation (which I hope is everyone!)' *Anvil*

cliff
COLLEGE
PUBLISHING
2004

ISBN 1 898362 32 7

A companion volume to

Mission and Spirituality – creative ways of being church

Mission and the Next Christendom